Bedrock!

Federalist No. 86

Bedrock!

Fixing the Foundation of America's Destiny

by Publius MMX

Recovering Federalist, LLC

ISBN 978-0-9845512-0-0

Printed in the United States of America.

"There are a thousand hacking at the branches of evil to one who is striking at the root."

—*Henry David Thoreau*

Contents

Foreword

"Any nation that expects to be ignorant and free expects something that never was and never will be."

"[Based on] the Laws of Nature and of Nature's God. . . . We hold these truths to be self-evident, that all men are created equal, that they are endowed by their Creator with certain unalienable Rights, that among these are Life, Liberty and pursuit of Happiness."

"Watch your thoughts, for they become words. Watch your words, for they become actions. Watch your actions, for they become habits. Watch your habits, for they become character. Watch your character—even as a nation—for it becomes your destiny."

"Whether we and our politicians know it or not, Nature is party to all our deals and decisions, and she has more votes, a longer memory, and a sterner sense of justice than we do."

"In the end nature always wins. As individuals, families, communities, states and as a country we have to stop trying to manipulate natural consequences, and get back to adhering to the Laws of Nature."

"Horse sense is the thing horses have that stops them from betting on people. . . . and against nature."

"Few will have the greatness to bend history itself; but each of us can work to change a small portion of events, and in the total, of all those acts will be written the history of this generation."

"Work without vision is drudgery. Vision without work is dreaming. Hope and vision coupled with work is DESTINY."

"There is only one road to freedom—*work!*"

Acknowledgments

First of all, we acknowledge and recognize the laws of nature and of nature's God.

We acknowledge divine providence and its hand in all things, including this effort. We understand that others may not, but regardless of whether we believe in God, lessons from history, Manifest Destiny, karma, or just plain ol' dumb luck, if we deny the laws of nature and their existence, we do so at our own peril—individually and collectively. We not only recognize those laws but also acknowledge a guiding hand in this work.

We also wish to acknowledge and recognize the founders of this great nation and those who framed the original debates—the Federalist/Anti-Federalist debate and other important debates that we desire to reignite with this work. We are truly concerned about our country and believe that time is of the essence for this discussion, which will continue with ongoing essays, books, and other works produced by Publius MMX, Recovering Federalist.

Preface

On September 17, 1787, the United States Constitution was adopted by the delegates at the Constitutional Convention in Philadelphia. Before the new Constitution could take effect, however, it had to be ratified by the states.

From the time the Constitution was signed by the delegates to the time it was finally ratified by the last state in 1790, a fierce national debate raged in the states regarding this great American experiment—the Constitution—and the new government it was intended to create. This debate occurred in meeting halls, on streets, and on the printed page. On both sides, heated argument was the order of the day, and both sides had a considerable following. Many of the questions raised at that time remain with us today: How should society be ordered? What is the proper role of government? What is the best form of government? What rights must governments protect? Which government powers should be held by the states, and which ones by the federal government? How can governments best be held accountable and in check?

From October 1787 to August 1788, a series of essays was published in New York newspapers and throughout the colonies with the goal of influencing the great debate. These essays, arguing for the adoption of the new Constitution, were a collaborative effort by several of the most prominent of the Founding Fathers of our nation. They wrote anonymously under the nom de plume "Publius," a name chosen in honor of the Roman consul and founder of the republic, Publius Valerius Publicola; a name that also means "friend of the people."

These essays laid the foundation for educating the public about the Constitution and provided a clear outline of the motivation and philosophy behind the proposed system of government. Along with a much smaller collection of rebuttal essays written under the pseudonyms

"Cato," "Brutus," and "Centinel," these essays played a crucial role in the ratification process.

Collectively, they became known as the *Federalist Papers.* The Federalist Papers are a fundamental part of our national heritage and remain a primary source for the interpretation of the U.S. Constitution today. The last essay in the series, published in August 1788, was Federalist No. 85.

This essay, *Bedrock!,* is Federalist No. 86. The purpose of this essay is to start to reexamine some of the questions posed in 1787, and in the ensuing Federalist Papers, and to reignite those debates. Writing under the pen name of *Publius MMX,* we pick up where the Federalist Papers left off, taking a fresh look based on conditions that exist today. We intend this to be the first in an ongoing series of essays, published with the subtitle *Federalist No. 86,* that take stock of where things stand in the United States today, addressing some of those same issues, and many of the other pressing core issues that trouble our country today, based on current conditions and circumstances. Our intent is to help open eyes and educate people about the challenges before us and, more important, to motivate us all to get involved and start participating in the process. After all, it's our life and our country—with no dress rehearsal.

We acknowledge that this is not a scholarly work. We do not claim constitutional expertise, nor do we claim to have all the answers. It is not our intention to debate theory or focus on many of the specific points of the original debate. Our goal is to open a new dialogue that can inspire thoughtful examination and motivated improvement, based not entirely on theory but on the actual conditions that have evolved over the past 200 years.

Although who we are and what we have done is of little consequence, our advantage in this discussion is one of perspective. We have seen the world and made things happen in both the private and public sectors. We have been on both sides of the table and both sides of the aisle. We have personal experience from the frontlines, the trenches of life's battles. We have experience navigating minefields—political minefields, regulatory minefields, and financial minefields, applying and experiencing actual application of the principles of the constitutions and governments of this country. Our experiences have been very sobering.

As Americans, we all now have 220 years of experience and *applied* theory to bring to the table as we move the debate forward. Rather than discuss abstract theory, we will talk mostly about our observations in the everyday world—our own experiences and those of others we have come to know—people such as Jacob Springer, Mancos MacLeod, Pearl Williams, Matt James, Maggie Rawlins, Benjamin Jakobs, Rosie McLayne, Nick Romero, and others who have assisted and provided real-life stories for this essay and the others we are working on. Stories of men like Worth Woolsey, a salt-of-the-earth rancher and treasure trove of sage advice and earthy wisdom. The stories are real, but the names and places have been changed to protect the anonymity and privacy of the parties involved. In Worth's words, "Political correctness be damned. As Americans, one thing we all need to clearly understand is that every single one of us has a dog in this fight, a horse in this race, and a stake in this discussion; it's our life and our future we're talking about."

In this book we focus the discussion almost entirely on domestic issues. We are throwing labels out the window. It is our intent to focus on principles, not personalities and associations. We don't want messengers to get in the way of the message. Correct principles are correct principles regardless of who states them.

If we can get past labels, we believe that there are basic, core, universal principles, based on the irrefutable laws of nature, that essentially everyone can and should agree on, regardless of their orientation—right, left, or center. As just one lighthearted, tongue-in-cheek example, consider for instance college football's BCS bowl system. Many of those familiar with the situation seem to agree with the basic premise that the current BCS bowl system needs to be replaced with a national play-off system. According to many, it's the only fair thing to do. Super Bowl XLIV and the 2010 NCAA Basketball Tournament clearly demonstrated why a play-off system would be a more fair and equitable approach, not to mention give us a glimpse of just how fun and exciting a play-off system in college football would be! Many argue that anyone looking at the situation objectively should be able to agree with this basic premise purely on its merits. But if someone like President Obama, for example, says it, a certain group of people will automatically and completely disagree, quit listening, and turn off the discussion once they see the source, on that basis alone; whereas another group of people will immediately agree and embrace the position on that basis alone. Sadly, this is also true with much more important principles.

To help avoid this, if a quote, story, or example fits the principle we're discussing, we're going to use it, as a general rule without any credits, citations, or references. We realize that this may seem unconventional, but what we're doing and how we're doing it is fairly unconventional to start with, so we're going to stick to principles and try to avoid letting labels, associations, and messengers get in the way or do our thinking for us. Writing anonymously as Publius MMX, we aren't concerned with taking credit, nor do we want who we are to get in the way of the message.

We believe this country is currently situated in such a way that time is of the essence. We know this and the other essays we are working on will not be perfect, either in form or content, but despite their imperfections we know the principles discussed, when applied, can and will make a difference for good. This work is a wake-up call and a call to action—a guide for taking stock of where we stand in the world today, taking basic steps to further strengthen the foundation of this great country, and correcting course as necessary.

It is our hope that this essay and those that follow will be the functional equivalent of Paul Revere on his midnight rides, waking up the countryside, calling the colonists to action, and calling revolutionary patriots to battle for freedom and liberty, to fight against tyranny and oppression of the British monarch.

We face similar challenges today. We need to start waking up and doing something about it—before it's too late.

General Introduction

Following the Boston Tea Party in 1773, there were running skirmishes between the colonists and the British until July 4, 1776, when the colonists openly rebelled against King George III by signing the Declaration of Independence. A grueling eight-year military conflict ensued. The Americans relied heavily on militiamen who were not sufficiently armed and had little formal training. Despite this and many other setbacks, the patriots were finally able to force the British general, Lord Cornwallis, to surrender at Yorktown, Virginia. The Americans had won the war. This great struggle for independence has come to be known as the American Revolution.

The journey to nationhood was not complete, however. Up to that point, the colonies had been operating under the Articles of Confederation, which had been adopted by the Second Continental Congress in 1775. After ultimately winning the war, the colonists were essentially left asking themselves "now what?" In 1785, some of the colonies reconvened to consider where to go from there and invited representatives from all the colonies to convene in secret in Philadelphia, starting in May of 1787.

The Constitutional Convention took place from May to September of 1787. After four long months of sweltering heat and humidity—and even more heated debate and deliberation—the delegates at last approved a final draft of the new Constitution on September 17, 1787. It had not been an easy task. Diverse agendas, personality conflicts, and regional differences all played a part. But in the end, compromises were reached, scores were settled, and the ultimate debate boiled down to the fundamental differences between two political camps: the Federalists and the Anti-Federalists.

Before the new Constitution could become law, it had to be ratified by at least nine of the thirteen states. Any state that voted *not* to ratify the Constitution would not be part of the new union and would remain an independent sovereign nation. Once the Constitution was adopted by the Philadelphia Convention, the campaign for ratification by the states continued, the debate among the people began in earnest, and the Federalist versus Anti-Federalist debate intensified.

What *was* the debate between the Federalists and the Anti-Federalists? Despite our objective to avoid labels, it is not entirely possible as we explore this particular debate.

The Federalist/Anti-Federalist Debate

Ratification of the Constitution by the states was by no means certain in 1787. Indeed, many people at that time opposed the creation of a federal, or national, government that would have power *over* the states. These people were called *Anti-Federalists.* They included, primarily, members of the middle class who were less likely to be a part of the wealthy, aristocratic elite than were members of their opposition, who called themselves Federalists. Anti-Federalist leaders included some of our most revered Founding Fathers, including leading national figures during the Revolutionary War period. Other Anti-Federalists were local politicians who feared losing power should the Constitution be ratified.

The Anti-Federalists believed that government generally should be founded on principles of self-government and self-sufficiency. They believed in a sustainable and self-sufficient society of productive, self-governing citizens, including farmers, tradesmen, and businessmen, who would participate as citizen lawmakers in representative government at all levels. Although the states would be part of a sovereign union, they believed each state should have a sovereign, independent government. Anti-Federalists also felt that increasing urbanization, commercialization, and centralization of power would lead to a number of problems in society, including eventual tyranny and oppression.

Federalists, on the other hand, came primarily from the wealthy, aristocratic class of merchants and plantation owners. They favored a centralized federal government that would govern the states as one large, continental nation. They supported government intervention in economic affairs and the creation of a national banking system.

Although ultimately compromises were made and some degree of balance was struck between the two sides, it was the Federalists who were most successful in having their goals met in the new Constitution. Between September 1787, when the Constitution was signed at the Philadelphia Convention, and May 1790, when Rhode Island became the last state to ratify the Constitution, the debate between the Federalists and the Anti-Federalists raged on. The Federalists argued that the new Constitution was a much-needed improvement upon the Articles of Confederation, the country's first attempt at unification, but the Anti-Federalists feared that the new, national government would seize the power of the states and the people, and they saw no sense in abolishing the existing administration for an entirely new and untested form of government.

In making their arguments, Anti-Federalists claimed that the Constitution represented a departure from the goals of the American Revolution and a move toward the twin evils of monarchy and aristocracy. In the new Constitution, they feared that the president was given too much power and the Congress had too few representatives for too many people. They also protested the lack of a Bill of Rights enumerating and protecting certain basic, inalienable rights that existed in the laws of nature and preexisted and preempted the Constitution or any other man-made legislation or entity.

The Anti-Federalists also asserted that a country as large and diverse as the United States could not possibly be effectively governed by one national government and that the new Constitution would ultimately spell an end to all forms of self-rule by the states. One Pennsylvania Anti-Federalist, who signed his articles "Centinel," declared,

"It is the opinion of the greatest writers, that a very extensive country cannot be governed on democratic principles, on any other plan than a confederation of a number of small republics, possessing all the powers of internal government, but united in the management of their foreign and general concerns.... [A]nything short of despotism could not bind so great a country under one government."

The Federalists focused their arguments on the inadequacies of national government under the Articles of Confederation and the benefits of national government as formed by the Constitution. Their wealth and prominence gave them the advantage of influence, and following the signing of the Constitution, Federalist delegates quickly returned to their states to organize state ratification conventions. They also began penning works like the Federalist Papers and collaborating with the press to publish them at such a dizzying pace that the Anti-Federalists found it impossible to keep up.

The majority of these Federalist arguments are notable for their vocal opposition to what later became the Bill of Rights. The addition of a bill of rights to the Constitution was originally controversial because the Constitution, as written, did not specifically enumerate or protect the rights of the people. Rather, it listed the *limited* powers of the government and left all that remained to the states and the people. Some prominent Federalists argued that any such enumeration, once written down explicitly, could later be interpreted as a list of the only rights that people had. In response to this assertion, in so-called Anti-Federalist No. 84, "Brutus" argued that government unrestrained by such a bill could easily devolve into tyranny. Other supporters of the bill argued that a list of rights would not and should not be interpreted as exhaustive; that these rights were merely examples of important rights that people had, but that people had other rights as well. People in this school of thought were confident that the judiciary would interpret these rights in an expansive fashion.

Lacking the affluence and dominion of the Federalist movement, the Anti-Federalists were not able to mobilize as quickly. In addition to getting the jump in delegate seats, the Federalists also got a clear and overwhelming advantage in the written debate waged in the Federalist/Anti-Federalist Papers. Consequently, though their influence was felt in many states, the Anti-Federalists were not able to sufficiently impact the ratification debate and muster enough votes to defeat ratification. The Anti-Federalist outcry, however, was not ultimately without its effects. The lack of a bill of rights proved to be a very thorny issue, and several states refused to ratify the new Constitution without it. As a result, before the ratification process was complete, the Bill of Rights was added to specifically address and protect certain inalienable rights bestowed by the irrefutable laws of nature as part of the first ten amendments to the Constitution, and those rights have become an important part of the United States Constitution and its heritage of liberty.

Chapter 1

Why the Federalist/Anti-Federalist Debate Is Still Relevant Today

When Rhode Island ratified the United States Constitution in 1790, it effectively decided the Federalist/Anti-Federalist debate. The discussion lives on, however, and now, more than two hundred years later, we face many of the same arguments that were contested then. The Tenth Amendment to the Constitution asserts that the states and the people reserve all powers not explicitly granted to the federal government. The Fourteenth Amendment, which was added after the Civil War, declares that no state can pass legislation infringing upon the constitutional rights of individuals, and that no individual can be deprived of life, liberty, or property without due process of law. The conflicts between these two amendments make up much of our political debate today. In the Constitution itself, the Supremacy Clause states that the Constitution is the "supreme law of the land" and must be upheld even if state laws or constitutions contradict it. The Commerce Clause has been interpreted and applied so broadly that today virtually nothing falls outside its scope. How do the Tenth and Fourteenth Amendments relate to these clauses? Our intent is to explore the critical differences between the constitutional republic the Founding Fathers envisioned and intended and the mob rule democracy that we have today. Entire new dimensions and branches of government that our Founding Fathers—including the Federalists—never contemplated have been created. The unintended consequences of those developments leave open the question of how, and by whom, this country is actually best governed today.

Federalism is an old concept and term whose meaning and usage has changed and evolved over time and is not clearly and universally understood today. According to the concept as debated originally, the term Federalism represented the concept of a strong *central,* national—federal—government and federal *supremacy* and dominance in the hierarchy of national government and relationship with the states and the people. The Anti-Federalists were the strong proponents of states' rights, a representative republic, a dual sovereignty system, and paramount protection of inalienable individual rights. Even the Federalists, however, sought a *healthy* balance between the states and the federal government.

Since then, however, the concept has evolved, and for a variety of reasons, the term Federalism and associated usages have become much more confusing. Although it seems counterintuitive, today many politicians, policy wonks, and academics use the term *Federalism* to mean exactly the opposite of what it originally represented—often associating the term with a stronger states' rights position and philosophy. Both in terms of what the general concept of Federalism meant in the original Federalist/Anti-Federalist debate and what it means to average, everyday American citizens today, this is very confusing and makes little sense. Moreover, at this point, even someone like James Madison, who is often called the "Father of the Constitution" and is one of the original deans of the Federalist position and author of many of the Federalist Papers, is undoubtedly writhing in his grave over how the concept of Federalism, even as he envisioned it, has mutated and evolved over the years, and how out of balance our "Federalist" system has now become.

Consequently, for purposes of this discussion and this essay, we are returning to the fundamental substance of the term as used and discussed by the Federalists and Anti-Federalists in the original debate and as it makes most sense to most average people today. For purposes of this essay, this discussion, and the essays that will follow, it represents the concept of a strong central government, federal supremacy and dominance—federal dominion—in our government's relationship with *we the people* and the states in this union—this federation—of united states. For purposes of this discussion, the term Federalism will also represent the concept that government—particularly the federal government—should play a dominant role in our society, and that government can and should take primary responsibility for many aspects of our lives, thus minimizing the need for, and fundamental role of, personal responsibility.

On that basis, inevitably, some will assert that, if anything, this essay and those that follow should have been subtitled *Anti*-Federalist No. 86. But like essentially everyone in this country, we are, in fact, Federalists, or at least *Recovering* Federalists. We are products of Federalism (according to our definition—federal dominion), sons and daughters of federal dominion. We have been eating the fruits and drinking the fine wines of federal dominion our entire lives. Like most Americans over the course of the past hundred years, we have drunk deeply of this federal dominion port and liked the taste. Being raised on it from the beginning, we have become addicted and dependent. Consequently, we are not writing from an Anti-Federalist viewpoint with an "I told you so" attitude. We are writing as sober, Recovering Federalists—as men and women with real-life experiences with federal dominion and real-life concerns about the state of the State and the future of the fat banquet we have enjoyed. It has been a great party and a great ride, but we must now seriously ask ourselves how much longer it can last—especially on the present course—and what it will ultimately look like if it does. At this point, we have come to see the truth of our fine federal dominion wine: that while there may be nothing wrong with a glass or two of federal power and dominion with dinner, or maybe even one with lunch, when we all start the morning with a full bottle and add to it from there, it poisons our system. And as with all addictions, we must first acknowledge that there is an issue—that we are indeed dependent—before we can empower ourselves to take action and do something about it.

To that end, it is time to start an organization—a movement—for a country grown weak on out-of-balance federal dominion. It is time to develop a rehabilitation program—a twelve-step process for *Recovering* Federalists—and it begins with sobering acknowledgment. We have come to acknowledge, and to encourage others to acknowledge, that there is serious concern with our current state of dependence—that there is a real need to change our present course.

Surprisingly, many of the original colonists in early America were apathetic about their government. According to some estimates, as few as 13 percent of the total population of the original colonies were actual revolutionary patriots—rebels—who risked all in support of the revolution. Likewise, only 7 to 15 percent remained loyal to the king throughout the war. Regardless of which side of the conflict they were on, by all accounts not more than 45 percent of those early Americans expressed allegiance or support for whatever form their government might take. *Well over half of the population were fence-sitters, willing to idly stand by and watch what their country might become.* Unfortunately, the prevalence of apathy is even worse today. Americans have grown—or continue to be—idle, docilely watching as our current situation continually deteriorates.

We are determined to purge our personal apathy. We hope this work will be an action guide. We encourage all who read it to join us as we resolve to take time out of busy lives to reflect on our history and, even more important, to ponder our future, to examine where we are in this country, to acknowledge the good and right as well as the things not quite right. We will discover how we arrived at this point. And finally, most important, we resolve to turn our focus to what can be done to restore our great, intended destiny. We are willing to take action. We are committed to strengthening the foundation of this great country. We are ready to help correct our course.

Chapter 2

What Is Right with America

America: land of the free, home of the brave! There are so many great things about our country that it is impossible to even consider listing them all. Here in America we have the right and the ability to be the absolute masters of our own destiny. In this country, through hard work, vision, thrift, and perseverance, anyone can "make it." Anyone can go as far and do as well as he or she wishes. Everyone has a chance to ring the bell, to hit the home run. This country is a place where opportunity and preparation can meet in such a way that anyone can "get lucky"—perhaps more so than anywhere else in the world. America is a place where anyone can get an education. It's a place where anyone can produce. A place where we can all reap what we sow. A place where anyone can succeed or fail and rise from the ashes to try again.

In the United States we have rights and freedoms that are completely unknown in many parts of the world. One of the greatest things about America is the unprecedented freedom of choice we have. While recognizing that this freedom has become progressively more limited in the passing decades, we believe there is still no other place on earth that offers more freedom of choice than we have here. We can choose where to live; we can choose our friends and affiliates; we can choose where and how to worship. We have free access to an infinite amount of information that we can choose to use as we wish. We can say anything we want. We get to choose how to make a living, where to go to college, what to eat, how to dress, whom to marry, when and how many children to have, and how to raise them. We get to choose our leaders and our partners. We even get to help choose the winner of *American Idol.*

America is a place where Cinderella stories can, and actually do, happen. Over half of the millionaires in this country are self-made with first-generation money. Whether we agree with President Obama's policies or not, we recognize that America is a very special, unique place where a young, mixed-race man with relatively little experience—a man without apparent privilege and without a high-profile family or background—can rise to the highest elected office in the land. America may be one of the only places in the world where that same man, who just a few years earlier was sporting worn-out shoes and reportedly had to borrow money to attend his own party's political convention, could turn around his own personal fortunes—first winning state, then national elections, writing best-selling books, and eventually raising more than a billion dollars in campaign contributions—to succeed in being elected president of the United States and becoming one of the most powerful men in the world. Amazing things can, and do, happen in America.

America is a chosen, promised land, hewn from a fertile wilderness, preserved by those who came before us, and inhabited by a people of rich heritage and great fortitude. Her beautiful, diverse landscapes, so blessed with natural resources and abundant productivity, are also home to amazing, scenic beauty and natural wonders.

One of the great strengths of this nation is and has always been our families and churches. At one point during the height of the industrial revolution, a notable foreign leader recognized that America's greatest strength came not from our steel mills, factories, or government, but from our churches and families, the most efficient and caring support systems our society has. Immigrant families and their descendants, operating in accordance with a legal framework that has allowed them to become citizens, keeping the best traditions that each family has, and sharing these while learning from the traditions of others has created a backbone of strength in America for generations. Churches, operating as an independent welfare branch, help people in ways governments simply are not capable of, free of state leadership and intervention.

Finally, one of the greatest things that is right with this country is the simplicity of our Constitution. After months of debate at the Constitutional Convention, our entire system of government was set up with a simple, seventeen-page document. Today you can hardly buy a home or car or even have an employment contract with only seventeen pages. But those pages sought to recognize and be in alignment with the laws of nature, or *natural law.* That alignment with the laws of nature has allowed Americans to advance more in every facet of the human experience since the Constitution's signing than any other people in the previous millennia. Why? Because we became free to dream, work, and make dreams a reality without interference from government. Free to build a business or an idea while focusing on the natural, consequential burden of a market that demands products of value, rather than the burden of bureaucratic control. Through the free will of a consumer, the market itself has dictated what should be produced, not a lord, king, dictator, bureaucrat, bishop, chancellor, or aristocrat. We-I-You have control of our destiny with little involvement from outside sources. We have been free to build a better mousetrap. But the question we have to ask ourselves is: *Is this still the case?*

Chapter 3

What Is Wrong with America—Just on the Surface

Obviously, there is a lot right with America. But it's not perfect; there are also problems. Unfortunately, many fundamental problems and issues have been pushed forward and "treated" by putting Band-Aids on symptoms, rather than addressing the real causes, for so long that it's starting to catch up with us. Problems that were once small have grown. Policies that were once ideas have become chains of bondage. The slow evolution from small hindrance to serious complication has gone on too long. This has happened for so many decades that it is getting difficult to keep acting as though these challenges are mere annoyances. The intent to fix things *later* is catching up. Tomorrow is upon us.

Again, focusing almost exclusively on domestic issues, what follows is a very quick, superficial sketch of just a few of the myriad problems that we see every day. We cannot address them all, but we'll call this a starting point.

Currently, the United States is nursing several popped economic "bubbles." We've been in the throes of a banking, credit, and financial crisis for at least the past two years. We have had a real estate meltdown and a housing crisis, and the great American automotive industry has been very wobbly. In short, we're experiencing the worst recession and financial downturn since the Great Depression.

So we've got some financial issues.

But they can be resolved with bailouts, right?

We're on solid footing otherwise, right?

Everyone else is doing fine, right?

We are still the strongest nation in the world, right?

The picture is painted for us. Regardless of economic hiccups, we still have strong values and moral character. The Great Recession is almost history. We are in full recovery. The bull has returned to the markets. We are still the economic superpower of the world. And any remaining tough economic numbers account for only a small part of the population. Indeed, things are looking up. Well, let's just take a real quick look at all that.

Today, despite our previous abundance and unprecedented prosperity, it is estimated that there are 3.5 million homeless people in this country, including approximately 1 million children. The "official" unemployment rate hovers right around 10 percent. If you count those who have quit looking for work or are underemployed, the number shoots past 20 percent, and in some places it's much worse. According to reports from one major mainstream media outlet, one in eight Americans is currently receiving food stamps, including as many as one in four children. As of February 2010, a leading nationwide title insurer estimated that 11.3 million homeowners owe more on their homes than they were worth at the end of 2009. That's nearly 24 percent of all homes that have a mortgage. According to another source, nearly half of the $1.4 trillion in commercial loans coming due over the next four years are underwater as well, with property values down as much as 40 percent in just the past two years. A recent study found American households lost $13 trillion in wealth between mid-2007 and March 2009. Today, less than 10 percent of our population owns more than 90 percent of the wealth and assets in this country.

We have voluntarily subjected ourselves to new forms of slavery. Let's face it: we're dependent. We consume more than we produce, individually and as a nation. We spend more than we make. We import more than we export. We're up to our ears in debt, both individually and as a country. Our current national debt is now more than $13 trillion dollars—that's $13,000,000,000,000. This is more than 86 percent of our total annual GDP. At this point, we're adding national debt at a rate of more than $250 billion per month. Individually, we're dependent upon banks and credit cards. As a country, we're financially dependent on foreign countries and the printing press. Our currency—the once-vaunted dollar—is no longer a sure bet. The "Fed" is printing money as fast as we can spend it, and the federal government is propping up our stock markets with its "PPT"—Plunge Protection Team.

On one hand, a great number of us are just living hand to mouth, paycheck to paycheck—just eating, sleeping, and going to work, really happy just to still have a job. On the other hand, even during the height of the downturn, Wall Street's biggest investment banks took advantage of all the opportunities to make record profits. Despite the uproar, they repeatedly *used* federal bailout money for lucrative bonus packages and have plans to further increase rewards for corporate management.

Beyond economics, in terms of domestic trends, the long-term crime rate is rising, and our children's test scores are falling. In the United States, with a divorce rate close to 50 percent, only 63 percent of American children grow up with both parents in the home, the lowest number in the Western world. Many couples never bother to get married, opting instead for a less-committed step of cohabitation. The number of children born out of wedlock is growing, and the abortion rate is growing even faster. Of the women who do commit to motherhood, 43 percent are raising children alone, either separated, divorced, or single. Clearly, the economic highs of recent decades have not made for bliss on the home front. In fact, sadly, even at the height of our most recent financial glory we weren't really happy, and many of us certainly aren't now as we struggle to keep our homes, families, and lifestyles afloat. And that's just talking about the rest of us. Completely disregarding all the celebrities of every other stripe, how many of our elected leaders have been tarnished by scandal and corruption? And our government—especially the federal government—is like a runaway train.

Our "good news" is that we have the cheapest, most readily available food supply in the world. But even this is tarnished by the real facts of our food system: agriculture in the United States has some real issues, and 99 percent of our population is completely dependent upon the 1 percent (in this country) who produce the food and agricultural products we consume.

Although we have been richly blessed with abundant natural resources, completely aside from pressing current circumstances in the Gulf of Mexico that only further emphasize this issue generally, our track record for resource stewardship is hardly something to brag about. And we're long overdue for a serious discussion about sustainability. In terms of basic necessities, including food, water, clothing, shelter, energy, and so forth, at this point our nation is no longer self-sufficient. This is the case both individually and collectively. In many areas, we already consume far more than we produce, yet our productivity continues to wane.

Consequently, despite all the spin we see and hear to the contrary, many of us still have that nagging feeling in the pits of our stomachs. We know instinctively that all is not right, that there is more to the equation than meets the eye, that eventually there is another shoe to drop.

Regardless of whatever silver linings can be found, unemployment rates are still phenomenally high, with some sources estimating the unemployment rate of young people aged thirty and under at over 25 percent. Although the bulls have supposedly returned, the markets are still very shaky, fragile, and scared. When one fat-fingered keystroke can result in the complete evaporation of over a trillion dollars of equity in one afternoon for no apparent substantive reason, in the process scaring the bejeebers out of the markets and leaving the global financial system wondering (as it has been wondering way too much lately) if the whole thing is going to get sucked into the abyss, we have every reason to be asking more questions. When one little glitch like that can send gold spiking to all-time highs and send crude oil plummeting over 20 percent in a week's time, what can we read between the lines?

And California, one of our "biggest" states, which has actually had the eighth largest GDP in the world, is completely underwater with no hope in sight. Arizona, Illinois, Nevada, New York, and nearly a dozen other states are right behind. And Detroit, that great city that just twenty to thirty years ago was considered a global model for efficiency, automation, and productivity, is now a poster child for failure and much of what is wrong with this country. Despite educational spending of more than $2,000 per student above the national average, the odds of a Detroit high school student's ending up in jail or prison are higher than the odds for that student's going to college.

One of our greatest concerns should be the political state of our nation. Aside from our many political leaders who are morally destitute, tarnished by scandal, corruption, and greed of all kinds, from sexual to financial or worse, the system itself—a two-party monopoly run by professional politicians and the would-be political elite—is plumb busted. Mainstream media would have us believe that our country is deeply divided over core political issues—that we all stand either with the Red or the Blue—when in reality, as many as 60 percent of us identify ourselves as independents. According to one commentator, "In the past year, our sitting president's approval ratings have fallen farther and faster than any president since Ford pardoned Nixon. While the *other* party obviously rejoices at such news, they should note that nearly half of the American people currently want *neither* of the two major political parties to control Congress, and approximately the same number want *all* incumbents, regardless of party, voted out of office—and for good reason." But how many independent or third-party candidates have any opportunity to get elected in today's political arena? When was the last time the mainstream media gave an independent or third-party candidate any meaningful exposure?

Despite our abundance and high standard of living, we have developed a serious national health crisis. Obesity is reaching epidemic proportions—to the point that our country's First Lady has called it a *national security threat.* According to the American Diabetes Association, more than 23 million children and adults in the United States have diabetes. It is estimated that end-of-2009 research statistics will report that one in four children will be diagnosed with early-onset diabetes. It is the seventh-leading cause of death in the United States and accounts for $174 billion per year in medical costs. The American Cancer Society estimates more than 1.4 million new cancer cases were diagnosed in 2009; heart disease affects 39 percent of American males; one in three Americans has high blood pressure, and the list goes on. As a result of collusion and the lack of true market competition, health care costs in this country are skyrocketing and insurance premiums are out of reach for many families. The U.S. Census Bureau has estimated that more than 45 million people (roughly 15 percent of the population) can't afford, or choose not to buy, health insurance and have very limited access to health care. The biggest reason people don't have health insurance is because they simply can't afford it. Yet Congress has just passed legislation that deprives them of their freedom of choice and forces them to buy health insurance, whether they can afford it or not, and penalizes them if they don't. Instead of looking around and saying, "We've got quite enough on our financial plates to deal with right now; let's get some of the rest of this under control before we tackle healthcare," Congress chose instead to multiply the financial woes for Americans, both individually and collectively. As costs rise in virtually every area, many Americans are simply running out of places to cut back.

Next on the list to take a quick pass under our microscope is the justice system. On the criminal side of the equation, both *real* and *swift* justice is very rare. Our prisons are overcrowded with repeat offenders. In fact, one in every one hundred adults in our country is incarcerated in our prison system, the highest incarceration rate and number of prisoners in the world. Yet guilty thugs routinely go free, and our posh prisons obviously serve as little deterrent to crime. On the civil side of the equation, whoever can last the longest (the party with the most money) usually wins. Insane tort awards take away all personal responsibility, while average people have little meaningful access to the system. Yet attorneys flourish, encouraging irrational suits, prolonging litigation, and inflating cases and court costs. In fact, the country is overrun with lawyers who make things more complicated than they need to be, create problems just so they can bill us to fix them, and work tirelessly to convince us that we can't live without them. (And lest anyone think we're being particularly hard on the legal profession, as members of that profession, we know of what we speak!)

Between the health care and insurance industry conglomerates, Big Pharma, Big Oil, the military/industrial complex, and the legal profession, we can see the fruits of unbridled greed firsthand. Please forgive us—we know we've left out plenty of other industries whose companies also fall into this category. It seems to have become the standard mode of operation for big business in this country to conspire with government. We certainly are not antibusiness. We are just against business mated with government to create artificial markets and unfair competitive advantages. These acts are even more unfair—and certainly more serious—than the BCS conspiring to "rig" the national championship game in college football. Where is the conscience—especially in these even bigger, more important arenas?

Last but not least, we're scared and angry. Despite winning an unwinnable war of independence against Great Britain, surviving a bitter civil war, fighting two world wars, surviving the Great Depression, avoiding nuclear holocaust during the Cold War, producing the "greatest generation," developing the greatest economy in the history of the world, and emerging as the world's sole superpower in the past two decades, our country has become very vulnerable in a number of different ways previously thought to be impossible. We have become hated by much of the rest of the world. On 9/11 we came under attack on our own soil and lost nearly three thousand lives. Since then, we've overthrown at least two governments halfway around the world, spent eight years chasing terrorists around the globe, and fought insurgents on at least two fronts with no end in sight. During the course of all that, we as a people apathetically looked the other way while our leaders passed new laws seriously infringing our personal rights and liberties—all in the name of national security. Despite having the best technology in the world and spending hundreds of billions of dollars on the War on Terror, we still have leaky borders, and we're still vulnerable in many aspects.

Today, for the first time in history, a majority of Americans fear that our country has crested—that our children and grandchildren will not be better off than we have been. Perhaps worst of all, terror today doesn't just come from fundamental religious extremists from halfway around the world. It also comes from the increasingly heavy-handed methods of our own governments.

Many believe this country is now on the verge of bankruptcy—morally, financially, and productively. In addition to being heavily indebted and dependent, both individually and as a nation, many of us feel in our guts that even more is wrong. Yet surprisingly, many of us act like we have no idea how this happened. Everything was going fantastically; we were at the height of our glory just a few short years ago, and then suddenly this—all these problems. We feel completely blindsided by this whole thing, and now we are suddenly in over our heads. Many leaders or experts of one sort or another have said, "There is no possible way we could have seen this coming."

What is even sadder and scarier is that this list is just starting to scratch the surface. Virtually all the issues we have listed here are only the superficial problems. They are really just symptoms of the real problems. This cursory list doesn't even begin to talk about what is truly *wrong* with America today. We need to get past the surface. We need to see past all the spin that surrounds us—past the wide-eyed excuses of politics and big business—and take a closer look with a critical and unforgiving eye at the way things really are. Like an emergency room doctor with a fainting snakebite patient, we could take a superficial approach and offer smelling salts for his fainting or apply blush to mask his paleness, but in order to save him we must look closer. We must remove the poison and administer the antivenom. Instead of treating the superficial symptoms, we must identify and address the cause of the problems.

One of our most noted Founding Fathers said, "The sting of any criticism comes from the truth it contains." We are willing to accept the sting and face the truth of where we stand. We are ready to look past the symptoms and see the real problems. Next, we must explore how and why we got here—and decide what to do about it.

Chapter 4

How and Why Did This Happen?

In any meaningful discussion about how we got here, we need to be careful not to have our vision so clouded by the rose-colored glasses of so-called "patriotism" that we can't see the real issues. In truth, we do have some serious fundamental problems—major cracks in our foundation that will become catastrophic if not corrected.

We don't feel the slightest bit unpatriotic in saying this. We view it much like restoring a wonderful old house. If we see that the walls are cracking, the ceiling is water-stained and sagging, and the beautiful old hardwood floors are stained and uneven, we must be wise enough to inspect further. To patch the walls, paint the ceiling, and put a rug on the floor—without ever addressing the fact that the roof is leaking and the foundation is cracked and settling, putting stress on the entire structure—we address only the superficial symptoms and seek to make do with temporary cosmetic solutions. It is far better to undertake the effort to discover the true reality, however harsh, and address the core causes of the superficial issues we encounter at first blush. In fact, to identify and give voice to serious problems and underlying causes, we believe, is exactly what needs to be done.

We love our country and feel fierce loyalty toward it. But just as loving parents who want the best for their children must be able to make honest assessments and sobering acknowledgments, see their children for who and what they are, and correct them when necessary, so must we be willing to look realistically at the situation and acknowledge the need to redefine boundaries or correct course. Sometimes a reality check and some tough love are exactly what are needed most. What follows is part of that reality check.

Although there are plenty of problems, simply joining in the chorus of whining and complaining is not our objective. We believe in doing something to address the real issues. We believe in advancing solutions rather than spending all our time talking about the problems. Consequently, a substantial portion of this essay and those that follow will deal directly with solutions—real things that *you and I* can do to help address and fix the problems. We have reached the point in this country where cosmetic face-lifts simply won't suffice. If the foundation of our collective home has cracks, causing ripples throughout the structure, then there is no point in fixing the roof, painting the trim, or patching the cracks in the walls (putting more Band-Aids on symptoms) without first making more serious repairs. And the same way a shifting floor creates cracks in the walls, many of these greater, more fundamental problems go hand in hand. Many problems have been created and/or encouraged by government action. We have seen a direct cause-and-effect relationship among laws, policies, and regulations implemented by our governments and the resulting negative effects in our personal lives.

The Core Causes

How did this happen? How did we get to this point? The short, simple answer is gradually—very gradually. The more probing question is *why* did it happen? While the answer to this question can seem complex given the complexity of the issues, in reality the *answer* is rather simple: as a nation, we have quit recognizing and adhering to the basic "Laws of Nature and of Nature's God" revered in the Declaration of Independence. Our single biggest problem is that we have moved away from this natural and uncompromising foundation of our existence. Our country and its people have spent most of the past century trying to find ways to cheat, buck, manipulate, and get around the laws of nature. As a society, we have spent the past one hundred years or more trying to make water run uphill, and trying even harder to convince everyone that it is natural and fully sustainable to do so, based on any fleeting successes we may have achieved in the process. We have spent decades putting our superficial fixes on symptoms and pushing problems forward to another day, waiting for trouble to right itself despite idly watching its causes grow. It doesn't make any sense. We have foolishly ignored the laws of nature. Given our history, Manifest Destiny, and concept of a Promised Land, we have come to believe that we are above and immune from the realities of the laws of nature. But whether we believe in God, lessons from history, Manifest Destiny, karma, or just plain ol' dumb luck, we are not immune to these laws; we are subject to them, and they continually act upon us—individually and collectively.

What Are the Laws of Nature?

The laws of nature are what remain if we remove all man-made laws, values, and morals. They preexist all forms of government, no matter how primitive. They are truths that stand alone and stand through time, throughout any civilization, American or otherwise. They are the basic, foundational laws that govern our world and the universe we live in. The laws of nature are the bedrock of our existence.

For many of us, the laws of nature are familiar, but we have forgotten them. We may not be able to list them if called upon to do so, but when we hear them they ring true and are as familiar as the water we drink and the air we breathe. One of the first such natural laws is that eventually all truth becomes self-evident. For centuries the earth was believed to be flat, but eventually the truth became self-evident. This has been the case throughout our history and will continue to be so into our future as truth reveals itself. Although neither the laws of nature nor truth evolve, our understanding of them does, and truth will always be truth whether we recognize it or not. Historically, virtually all truth—including scientific truth—goes through three basic phases: first, it is ridiculed; second, it is violently opposed; third, and finally, it is accepted as being self-evident. As with truth, we may not yet fully know and understand all of the laws of nature, but we do know and understand at least some of them.

Basic Foundational Laws of Nature

It is impossible to list all of the laws of nature. The following is barely a beginning. For the sake of discussion, and to help us better understand these core principles, the concepts illustrated in this short list remind us that the laws of nature are constant and irrefutable.

- For every action there is an equal and opposite reaction.
- Everything on earth is subject to the law of gravity.
- All things naturally tend to take the course of least resistance—water runs downhill.
- All existence is based on, and subject to, natural cycles.
- Neither the earth nor the human race nor the USA is the center of the universe.

These few examples are just the tip of the iceberg in terms of explaining the fundamental laws of nature. There are many other laws that we know and understand—and many that we may not fully know or understand yet. Our very existence is subject to these irrefutable natural laws.

But how do the laws of nature apply to us? What does a law such as "an object at rest tends to stay at rest; an object in motion tends to stay in motion" mean to us in everyday terms? Simply put, it means that momentum is a real factor in our lives. It means when we get rolling on a course, we can expect things to keep rolling awhile. And it means that when we are stuck, it takes *a lot* to get us unstuck.

Before we really get serious about spelling out longer lists of specific natural laws that apply to a variety of situations, this next list includes some realistic and easily understandable statements of some self-evident and irrefutable natural laws in everyday terms that most of us will be familiar with.

Commonsense Statements of the Laws of Nature— in Everyday Terms

Here is a list of common interpretations of the laws of nature—an everyday translation of the commonsense laws that we all should recognize:

- All actions have consequences.
- Blame, like water, naturally runs downhill.
- There is no such thing as a free lunch.
- Good fences make good neighbors.
- Use it or lose it.
- Possession is nine-tenths of the law.
- It's hard to teach old dogs new tricks.
- Old habits die hard.
- The early bird gets the worm.
- If you snooze, you lose.
- Many hands make light work.
- Young children have more energy than their parents.
- Parents have more knowledge and wisdom than children.
- Hardships and challenges are good for character.
- What doesn't kill you only makes you stronger.
- You don't get something for nothing.
- The more we get, the more we want.
- There are exceptions to every rule—and exceptions to the exceptions.
- Easily obtained, lightly esteemed—if you do get something for nothing (or next to nothing), there is a natural tendency not to appreciate and take care of it.
- Two wrongs don't make a right.
- Even reasonable minds can disagree.

- Most people go along just to get along.
- Bad things happen to good people too.
- It's a tough/dirty job, but *somebody*'s got to do it.
- Panic only makes things worse.
- You can't have your cake and eat it too.
- If you spend more than you make, you're broke.
- If you consume more than you produce, you're dependent.
- If you borrow more than you can pay, you're going to lose something.
- Expect the unexpected.
- Just because something has never happened yet doesn't mean it never will.
- While the sun shines is the time to save for a rainy day—when the time of need arrives, the time for preparation is usually past.
- If you treat people poorly, they aren't going to like you.
- Hindsight is twenty-twenty.
- It's always harder to go back.
- Free markets are based on supply and demand.
- What goes up must come down.
- The bigger they are, the harder they fall.
- Small leaks and loose lips sink big ships.
- Failure is a natural prerequisite to success—practice makes perfect.
- Nothing stays the same—it's either moving forward or sliding backward.
- Nothing is as constant as change.

- Change can be as good as rest.
- Delayed gratification pays.
- Government that governs least governs best.
- Nothing (man-made) lasts forever.
- Don't judge others until you have walked in their shoes.
- You can't take it with you.

The list could go on and on. This lighthearted sampling of everyday interpretations of the laws of nature could apply to everything. They repeat their lessons throughout our lives, over and over. They are commonsense principles, time-tested and self-evident. They include and offer more natural wisdom than is available in most university graduate degree programs. They apply to individuals; they apply to nations. Obviously these principles apply to us here in the United States. Because they are universal, they also apply to every other nation on earth. But sometimes we believe we can change the rules. We pretend they don't apply to us or that we can find a way around them. Possible? Maybe, for a time. Although there are exceptions to every rule, the idea that what goes up can stay up forever is a flawed one. The plan to get something for nothing rarely works out. No matter our schemes, we are not exempt from the fundamental laws of nature.

Laws of Nature Applicable to the Relationship Between Living Things and Resources

One of the fundamental laws of nature is that everything on earth is created and exists for a purpose. All things are intended to be put to beneficial use, to fulfill their purpose. Laws of nature apply not only to humans and their actions but also to all living things, resources, and their relationships to each other. Some related laws that apply to the relationship between living things and resources include the following:

- All species are perpetuated by natural selection—survival of the fittest.

- Animal species survive and thrive by their own efforts.
- Not all resources are in infinite supply—although they are renewable given enough time and the right conditions.
- Not all species are created equally—there is a food chain.
- Human beings have dominion and stewardship over all things on the face of the earth.

Certain laws apply specifically to human beings. The founders of our nation recognized these laws and made note in the Declaration of Independence of the "Laws of Nature and of Nature's God." Expressly acknowledging that there are more such principles, the founders made specific reference to just a few that govern human relationships. According to the founders, certain truths—founded upon the laws of nature—are self-evident. Among those laws the founders considered to be self-evident, and of particular relevance to the citizens of this country, were "all men are created equal . . . endowed by their Creator with certain unalienable Rights, that among these are Life, Liberty and the pursuit of Happiness—That to secure these rights, Governments are instituted among Men, deriving their just powers from the consent of the governed,—That whenever any Form of Government becomes destructive of these ends, it is the Right of the People to alter or to abolish it, and to institute new Government, laying its foundation on such principles and organizing its powers in such form, as to them shall seem most likely to effect their Safety and Happiness."

Laws of Nature that Apply Specifically to Human Beings

In the spirit of the statements made by our Founding Fathers, this list of the basic, self-evident laws applies particularly to human beings and their relationships with each other and other living things and resources.

- Human beings are specially endowed with the power of reason.

- Human beings are specially endowed with freedom of choice—otherwise known as liberty—subject to natural consequences. Such fundamental freedom of choice naturally includes decisions as to family, friends, associates, location, worship, education, livelihood, expenditure of time, energy, resources, and so forth.

- Human beings, based on their natural power of reason and freedom of choice, have unlimited capacity to learn, change, and adapt.

- Although human beings are not all created equally, they are created as equals—regardless of their race, color, caste, creed, gender, natural gifts, talents, or assets.

- Human beings are personally responsible for themselves, their offspring, and their families.

- Human beings are naturally entitled to be the masters of their own destiny with the right and freedom to survive and thrive according to their own efforts.

- Human beings are entitled to life, liberty, and the pursuit of happiness.

- Human beings acquire private ownership of property by putting their time, efforts, and other resources at risk to put new resources to beneficial use and by exchanging value with other human beings who claim prior ownership of the property subject to exchange.

- When human beings acquire private ownership of property by putting their time, efforts, and resources at risk, by nature they will exercise their innate freedom of choice to enhance, improve, defend, and make that property better and more productive and valuable.

- Human beings are naturally entitled to defend themselves, their families, and their inalienable liberties and rights, including property, from all attacks and intrusions.

- Those who are capable have the natural and inherent obligation to protect and defend those who are defenseless.

- Human beings are entitled to govern themselves entirely and without interference unless their self-governance interferes with someone else's equal freedom of choice and right of self-governance.
- Greed is a natural tendency among humans—the more they get, the more they want.
- Humans also have a natural tendency to think the more they have, the better they are; consequently, the natural lust or desire for money also has a natural tendency toward corruption.
- Human beings are accountable for their actions—especially as they relate to others.
- No person can be an impartial judge in a conflict or controversy in which he or she is a party.
- Human beings must learn to crawl before they can learn to walk, must learn to walk before they can learn to run. Failure is a natural prerequisite to success; practice makes perfect.

Of the laws of nature that apply to human beings, there are certain laws that apply specifically to families and their roles in society and perpetuating the human race.

- Family is the core unit of human existence and society.
- Men are naturally endowed to be protectors.
- Women are naturally endowed to be nurturers.
- The human race can be naturally perpetuated only by men and women mating and producing children.
- Families have a primary, personal responsibility to educate, care for, and provide for their own, and to govern themselves.

These basic laws of nature make sense. They are ideal, guiding principles for self-governance. Society is not always so cleanly ordered, however, and inevitably, once our relationships become such that it is necessary to move beyond self-governance, the laws of nature become a little more complex.

Basic Laws of Nature that Apply to Human Government

When self-governance is no longer enough and a societal government is put into effect, the laws of nature must again be the guiding principles in order for governments to be successful in honoring the rights of the society. The laws of nature, especially those pertaining to common government and the natural tendencies of those who govern, should be acknowledged and accommodated for. Such laws include:

- Common government and resulting laws are instituted only for application to those situations where individuals fail to satisfactorily govern themselves.
- Laws are instituted to deter and provide consequences for the violation of these and other laws.
- Laws limiting self-governance should exist only by consent of those governed by such laws.
- Those chosen to lead and govern others should be chosen by the people to be governed. In cases where there is not unanimous consent as to who should govern, it should be determined by the majority.

- Those chosen to lead and govern others are naturally obligated to act in the best interest of the people they are governing, subject to the laws of nature.
- When the best interests of people conflict, the interests of a majority of the people should be protected, subject to the laws of nature, including protection of inalienable rights, which should not be infringed regardless of what the majority may say or the size or strength of the majority.
- It is the natural disposition of almost all men that, as they get authority, they will begin to exercise unjust dominion.
- When people are given power over others, the natural tendency is to begin to advance their own self-interests ahead of those governed; to exercise greater power and control than necessary, resulting in unjust dominion—and the longer they are in power, the more difficult it is to resist these tendencies. In other words, power has a natural tendency to corrupt.
- The governed are entitled to know what their leaders are doing and have input in the process.
- Regardless of any man-made laws to the contrary, those chosen to lead and govern others are subject to applicable laws of nature and are directly accountable to those they govern.
- When human beings create a government, they have an obligation to support the core functions of government, both financially and through service. But the resulting government is likewise obligated to protect, defend, and preserve fundamental individual rights, including life, liberty, and property.
- Government that governs least governs best.

In one of our following essays, *Enough!*, we will focus on application of laws of nature to human government. It will start by addressing the natural consequences and cycles of human government, based on the laws of nature and the lessons of history. Then it will explore where we stand today in those natural cycles.

Well-known Sayings, Fables, and Stories Based on Natural Law

Consider for a moment many of our age-old bits of wisdom: a stitch in time saves nine; an ounce of prevention is worth a pound of cure; haste makes waste; don't bite off more than you can chew; live within your means; a penny saved is a penny earned; measure twice, cut once; plan your work and work your plan; you reap what you sow; by their fruits ye shall know them; if at first you don't succeed, try, try again. These and many more wise and familiar sayings are based on fundamental principles of the laws of nature.

One of the most applicable stories is about the camel that wanted to stick its nose in the tent. According to this tale, one cold night, as an Arab sat in his tent, a camel gently thrust his nose under the flap and looked in. "Master," he said, "let me put my nose in your tent. It is cold and stormy out here and the air is full of dust." "By all means," said the Arab, "and welcome." And he turned over and went to sleep. A little while later the Arab awoke to find that the camel had not only put his nose in the tent but his head and neck also. The camel, who had been turning his head from side to side, said, "I will take but little more room if I place my forelegs within the tent also. It is difficult standing out here." "Yes, you may put your forelegs within," said the Arab, moving a little to make room, for the tent was small. Finally, the camel said, "May I not stand wholly inside? I keep the tent open by standing as I do." "Yes, yes," said the Arab. "Come wholly inside. Perhaps it will be better for both of us." So the camel crowded in. The Arab, with difficulty in the crowded quarters, again went to sleep. When he woke up the next time, he was outside in the cold and the camel had the tent to himself.

We don't have to look hard to find situations where this fable applies. How many times have we felt left out in the cold as government in general and a wide variety of policies, laws, and regulations take over our daily affairs bit by bit? And what good purpose have these policies actually served? What good works have they accomplished?

We all know the story of the little red hen, who found some grains of wheat that none of her friends would help her sow, water, thresh, grind, or bake into bread. But when it came time to eat the bread, they were all eager for it. "I found the wheat," she told them. "I planted it, I weeded it, and when it was time to harvest it, I did that too. I took it to the mill to be ground into flour and, at last, I baked it. And now," said the little red hen, "because of my efforts, I have bread. Now I am going to eat it." And she did.

Tales such as these were not told purely for entertainment. These stories have been retold for generations because of the messages they hold. Just as the little red hen learned to be self-sufficient and hard working, in order to adhere to the laws of nature, we too must take responsibility for ourselves and our own progress. But just as many of us have begun to overlook these sayings and stories, we have also begun to ignore and underestimate the laws of nature they stand for.

Laws of Nature Are the Basis and Foundation for the Declaration of Independence, the Constitution, and the Bill of Rights

Many people have the mistaken understanding that the Constitution and the Bill of Rights create or grant rights, when in reality, fundamental, inalienable rights *already exist* based on the preexisting laws of nature. Those documents merely recognize them. The First Amendment clearly illustrates this point: "Congress shall make no law ... abridging the freedom of speech, or of the press; or the right of the people peaceably to assemble, and to petition the Government for a redress of grievances." Returning to the Federalist/Anti-Federalist debate, in light of this country's track record for not recognizing and acting in accordance with the self-evident laws of nature, what in all likelihood would have happened if the Bill of Rights had not been explicitly spelled out in those very first amendments to the Constitution, as the Anti-Federalists insisted? The Bill of Rights does not create these rights; it simply acknowledges them and others, such as the right to keep and bear arms, as *preexisting natural rights,* and it simply prohibits government from making any laws that infringe upon them.

Chapter 5

How Do the Laws of Nature Apply to Our Everyday Lives?

To help illustrate our points and show how the laws of nature apply to real-life situations, we've got some real stories and examples from the heartland.

The bedrock principles of the laws of nature—the bedrock of the bedrock—are freedom of choice (liberty) and personal responsibility. Unfortunately, these core universal principles are rapidly losing ground in the American consciousness.

The Wise Professor

On the subject of personal responsibility, which covers a broad spectrum with many different levels, our first story is about a wise college professor. According to the good professor, "Life is about choices and consequences" (it has now gotten to the point that we have to send our kids to college to learn this fundamental concept). This professor taught his students the importance of the decisions they make as to how they use their time, money, and resources. It was something he tried not only to teach but also to put into practice and pass on, by way of example, to his children as well as his students.

To help illustrate his point, he recalled an experience he had with his eight-year-old daughter as they were preparing to take a walk around the neighborhood. He told her to take a jacket because it was cold outside. "No, I don't need one," she insisted. He explained that she would get cold if she didn't have her jacket, yet she still maintained she didn't need one. "Okay," he said, and they went on the walk.

A few blocks into the walk she started grumbling about how cold it was and began rubbing her arms. What did the good professor do? Did he cut the walk short? Did he take off his own jacket and lovingly place it around his daughter? No, they finished the full walk, as intended, while she shivered and walked faster to stay warm. "Life is about choices and consequences," he explained to his daughter.

Sixty-plus years ago, people reading this would have said, "Well done; he taught his daughter a valuable lesson." But today, many reading this will inevitably cry: "Child Abuse!" "It was the father's fault for not *making* her take her jacket!" "You can't blame the daughter; she didn't know; she can't be held responsible!"

When and Where It All Begins

The college professor's story helps start this discussion, illustrates this principle in very simple terms, and explains when and where it all begins. As a natural progression in that discussion, a high school guidance counselor recently made this observation: "What happened to parents teaching their kids personal responsibility, including budgeting, waiting for things, and paying their obligations? Apparently that doesn't happen much these days. I talk to young people every day who believe that when they graduate from college (that someone else is supposed to pay for), they will be entitled to have a new house, bigger than their parents' home, and a starting salary close to $100,000. They seem to have no grasp that such ideas have no basis in real life. I have recently counseled young people who didn't know that not paying their bills could have a negative effect on their creditworthiness and their ability to purchase a car in the future. How can people, even teenagers, not know that? How can people, including teenagers, be so lacking when it comes to a fundamental grasp of personal responsibility? Somebody needs to teach them. What I want to know is how I got stuck with that assignment."

The Train Called Personal Responsibility

Our next story along this line comes a little farther down that path, from a different level and a different spot in the spectrum of personal responsibility. It comes from a juvenile probation officer who spends every day talking to young people who, for the most part, don't have the good fortune of learning such basic fundamental principles when they are young.

"My recent experience at the Vision Splendor Youth Rehabilitation Center seems to epitomize the recurring theme that has become the story of my life when it comes to dealing with the young people I work with. Despite the fancy name, Vision Splendor is a prison for kids, but it does have a striking view of the beautiful mountains nearby. In front it looks like a public school, but the grounds are surrounded by a high fence, with barbed wire along the top, and many of the heavy locked doors are also guarded.

"As I sat down to talk with one of the young people on my list, a sixteen-year-old boy, he only wanted to know one thing: 'What are you doing to get me out of here?' 'What are *you* doing to *help* me get you out?' I asked. We just kept asking each other the same questions over and over again. I suggested some options that required his cooperation and some acceptance of responsibility. He just kept saying, 'I don't belong here. . . . It wasn't my fault.'

"Vision Splendor has two parts. One part is for kids who have been committed by a judge until they are eighteen. The other part is for kids who have not yet been fully committed, but are sent for shorter 'shock sentences' to scare some sense into them. This young man has been a regular in court, never for anything really serious but always for somehow 'being in the wrong place at the wrong time' *because of what someone else did.* He is in the middle of his third, and longest, shock sentence. This is his last chance. He is very close to being fully committed until he becomes an 'adult.'

"His part of our conversation sounded like a broken record playing 'it's not my fault' over and over again, interrupted only occasionally by his insistence that he didn't want to be committed.

"Finally (exercising great patience and restraint), I calmly said, 'You know, just about everyone here, and almost every adult in prison, will tell you the same thing—it's not their fault. As long as they keep telling themselves that, and as long as you keep believing that, you're not learning a thing from this experience, and you're going to get stuck here, or in a place like this—possibly for the rest of your life. . . . You can get out of here, but there's only one way out; there's only one way home—it's on a train called *personal responsibility.*' By then, he was sobbing uncontrollably. After a few minutes, I continued, 'You cannot control what anyone else does, but you can control what you do, including your reaction to what other people do. You are completely responsible for your own actions, and the sooner you figure that out, the better off you're going to be. So it's time to grow up and take responsibility for your own life and the consequences of *your* actions.'"

Triple Homicide

Issues related to the acceptance of personal responsibility now pervade every level and aspect of our society. Our friend Mancos, a retired attorney, relates the final story that should help bring a basic understanding of this core principle full circle. This story is based on a case in his community that came to be known locally as the "triple homicide." The facts of the case are pretty simple. A local resident had several large dogs that frequently roamed the neighborhood and streets of town without restraint or supervision. On the occasion in question, the dogs got into a neighboring farmer's flock of sheep, injured many, and killed two. The farmer caught the dogs in the act and shot one of them—hence the triple homicide.

Rather than the dog owner taking responsibility for his dogs and the damage they had done, however, he sued the farmer, the town, the county, and the state for tens of thousands of dollars. According to the complaint and the evidence presented at trial—yes, believe it or not, the dog owner insisted on taking the case to trial—it was everyone else's fault: The farmer's fences were inadequate. The sheep were enticing the dogs. The farmer and his sheep were obsolete and out of place. As a developing suburban and residential neighborhood, the area should have been zoned to prohibit the keeping of farm animals and livestock. The farmer should have called animal control officers before taking matters into his own hands. Animal control officers should have prevented the dogs from killing the sheep. Applicable laws and ordinances did not adequately advise the dog owner that he was responsible for his dogs. And last, but certainly not least, both the farmer's and the town's liability insurance policies should cover not only the "damages" resulting from the loss of the dog but also pain, suffering, emotional distress resulting from the loss of the "man's best friend," and all attorneys fees and costs incurred by the dog owner to bring the case to trial.

In addition to being a good illustration of how far removed we have become from the bedrock principle of personal responsibility, this story also illustrates why good fences make good neighbors.

The Buck Stops Here

In this country, we have developed this very bad habit, individually and collectively, of always trying to find someone else to blame—someone else to take responsibility for the consequences of our decisions and actions. And we have developed the even worse habit of always wanting government to intervene to either force everyone to make the "right" decision and do the "right" thing, or to rescue us from the negative consequences of our bad decisions and irresponsible behavior.

As one prudent jurist has put it, "It is not the responsibility of the government or the legal system to protect a citizen from himself and the consequences of his decisions and actions. . . . You made a poor choice; take your lumps and move on."

This is a big part of how we have deviated from the fundamental laws of nature and what is fundamentally wrong with our society. We've become a people who want to blame everyone but ourselves, and we want someone (often government) to "make" us do the right thing because we don't want to take that responsibility ourselves.

According to some experts, "The acceptance of personal responsibility is what separates fully functioning adults from children. Responsibility is the hallmark of the fully integrated, fully functioning human being. It is the great leap forward into maturity. That thought is like a parachute jump—scary and exhilarating at the same time. It's one of the biggest and most important ideas that can ever occur to and take root in any of us." But it has evolved into one of the biggest deficits in our collective national psyche.

Contrary to what many have come to believe, once we become adults, because we have freedom of choice and personal responsibility and because we have chosen each and every circumstance of our lives, we are completely responsible for all of our own personal successes and failures, happiness and unhappiness, present and future. Responsibility goes hand in hand with success, achievement, motivation, happiness, and self-actualization. It's the absolute minimum requirement for the accomplishment of everything we could ever really want in life.

At the end of the day it's about taking a coat when it looks chilly outside. We can choose not to, it's true, but we shouldn't whine when we get cold. Life's about choices and consequences.

Failure Is a Prerequisite to Success—Practice Makes Perfect

As a natural consequence of our evolving aversion to personal responsibility, many of us have developed a huge, inherent fear of failure. What we fail to realize is that, as a general rule, failure is a prerequisite to success. According to Worth, "A smart man learns from his own mistakes; a really wise man learns from everyone else's." But in reality, the main way most of us learn—and the main way most people become wise in the first place—is by making lots of mistakes, experiencing failure, and taking something from those experiences. According to the title of one book on this subject, "the road to success is paved with failure." The reality is that many first-time successes are flukes.

Learning from Our Mistakes

Our main story on this point comes from Benjamin Jakobs, a newspaper cartoonist who helped us with some of the illustrations for this essay and those that will follow. According to Ben:

"Last fall my oldest daughter started college. As is customary, I told her I loved her and wished her success. But I wasn't telling the whole truth. While I do hope and wish for her ultimate success, I actually wish for her to experience plenty of failure along the way. I believe in the power of failure.

"In most instances, we learn little from our successes. In many cases, success is simply proving that we can do something we already know we can do, or 'getting lucky' and doing something correctly the first time, which can be problematic because first-time success is often a coincidence, or even a complete accident, and gives us the wrong idea of how things really work. First-time failure, by contrast, is expected; it is the natural order of things. Failure is how we learn.

"There is an old African phrase describing a good cook as 'one who has broken many pots.' If you've spent enough time in the kitchen cooking to have broken a lot of pots, you probably know what you're doing. My brother is a chef, and it's interesting to listen to a bunch of chefs when they get together. They tend to spend a lot of time comparing knife wounds and burn scars. Among their peers, they seem to know how much credibility their battle scars—and the mistakes and failures they represent—give them.

"Instead of handling sharp knives and scalding hot pans, I earn my living by drawing cartoons for a newspaper. After considerable experience, I still know that each week one of my pieces is going to be worse than all the others. It's not like I set out trying for that result; I do my best with every piece. But every week one cartoon is worse than the others, and sometimes very noticeably so.

"I have learned to treasure each of those 'worst' pieces. They become my battle scars. A 'successful' piece often means that I am largely using established techniques and doing things that I have done before—sticking with old tricks that I have practiced and perfected. Often in my inferior pieces, I am trying to pull off something new, something I've never done before, something I'm not even sure can be done. And that is where I learn by far the most. And this is true of virtually everything in life.

"My college student daughter, who has now successfully completed her freshman year, has been an aspiring perfectionist since the time she was very young. She feels her failures deeply, and I always want to comfort her. But in addition to comforting her, I hope I can always remind her of what she has learned from her failures and mistakes, and how she can do whatever it is better next time. It seems to be working because she takes it all in stride much better now than she did when she was in kindergarten. Back then, I couldn't tell her that failure is a good thing because that's not a lesson you can learn when you're five. But I did always tell her that it's not the end of the world. Indeed, with luck, every failure and mistake is just a beginning. Only practice makes perfect."

Universal Application in All Aspects of Life

This universal principle is also tried and tested in business. A well-known professor at Harvard Business School who has studied how organizations learn from failure says managers would do well to think more like scientists. "Failure provides more 'learning' in a strictly logical or technical sense than success," she says. "It's a principle of the scientific method that you can only disconfirm, never confirm, a hypothesis."

Failure's capacity to teach is exactly why venture capitalists often look for managers to run start-ups whose résumés include experience with a flop. With the right attitude, errors on the job, as long as they aren't repeated, should be valued. New research is pinpointing how we learn and make decisions. To the brain, a new thought or idea is like a spider. If it is industrious enough, an intricate web of knowledge spins out from it. Snapshots of the brain taken during learning actually show neurons firing, growing, and forming new connections. This is fascinating in itself, but what's even more fascinating is that failure can trigger this. That's right, failure enhances our brains. According to leading researchers in this area, "We always knew people could learn from their mistakes, but now we're finding out exactly how and where this happens. Basically, it all comes down to survival. In a normally functioning brain, failure is welcomed as an opportunity for learning and strengthening the species."

It is a fundamental law of nature.

If You Treat People Poorly, They Aren't Going to Like You

Another universal law that fits this same niche has to do with how we treat other people. Like many of us, Mancos had to learn this universal truth the hard way—primarily from mistakes and failure. Mancos started out his law practice in Flagstaff, Arizona. As a hotshot young attorney, he didn't waste any time trying to make his mark, and stepped on plenty of toes in the process. For whatever reason, he seemed to have a lot of pent-up anger inside and something to prove. He was more concerned about being right and winning at all costs than he was in being civil. Consequently, he was often overzealous in his actions. Although he won plenty of cases and arguments, and many of his clients liked his hard-nosed approach and resulting outcomes, other attorneys and even judges and staff began to detest working with him. The bottom line is, if you treat people poorly, they aren't going to like you. And it took awhile for Mancos to catch on. Although it is hard to teach old dogs new tricks and old habits die hard, as human beings, we do have the ability to learn from our mistakes as well as the freedom of choice and personal responsibility for who and what we are and how we behave. If something needs to change, we have the ability to change it.

Jake's First Landlord

When Jacob Springer was ready to rent his first apartment in a small community just outside Philadelphia, his new landlord told him: "I know your parents and your grandparents. I know you come from a good, responsible family. But I'm going to give you exactly the same spiel I give everyone: Rent is due on the first of the month. If you can't pay, move out. I know the law provides a three-day grace period, but if you can't pay, just get out because you're going to get an eviction notice. Don't bother with excuses; I've heard them all. The bottom line is, you don't get something for nothing. If you don't pay, there are natural consequences. If you don't pay, I can't pay my bills. If I can't pay my bills, I lose my house. And that doesn't make sense or do anybody any good because then we're both homeless. So pay your rent, and pay on time, and we'll all be happy."

Perhaps Jake's landlord seems harsh. After all, where's the compassion? What if there is a good reason that Jake can't pay his rent? What if Jake gets sick and can't go to work? What if he loses his job or the company he works for goes out of business? What if it isn't Jake's fault? Shouldn't the landlord exercise compassion? Shouldn't there be a law requiring him to help Jake out?

Let's think about this. If we pass a law that requires Jake's landlord to exercise compassion and let him stay in the apartment without paying rent, would that law violate any of the laws of nature? The first law of nature this would violate is the landlord's fundamental freedom of choice. If Jake doesn't pay his rent, his landlord should be able to exercise his freedom of choice to kick Jake out. The landlord is entitled to the rent, and Jake is not entitled to get something for nothing. Of course, freedom of choice is subject to natural consequences, and Jake might hate his landlord for kicking him out, but that's just one of those consequences. In all likelihood, however, the way Jake feels about his landlord will be based more on the way his landlord treats him, even the way he asks him to leave, than the actual eviction because Jake innately knows and understands natural law—you don't get something for nothing. When you can't pay your bills, regardless of the reason, you lose something, including a place to live. The landlord's actions are likewise subject to the laws of nature. If he is demeaning and insolent, Jake will resent him. After all, respect is an asset regardless of the necessity of eviction. But if the landlord does exercise compassion and lets Jake stay in the apartment without paying rent, he may not be able to pay his own bills. Therefore, he must do so only if he himself is able to afford Jake's rent. If not, then he too could lose his home due to nonpayment, falling subject, as we all are, to the ultimate mandate of that fundamental and irrefutable natural law that we simply don't get "something for nothing."

But is this an overly cynical outlook? Is there no room for compassion in the laws of nature? By all means. In fact, compassion thrives under these natural laws and is especially the role of families, churches, and charities, which we will discuss in more detail later. But is charity and compassion the proper role of government? We have to ask ourselves whether any governmental law requiring compassion is consistent with the laws of nature. Think about it. In real application, any such mandate would violate several natural laws. The first is freedom of choice. The second is you don't get something for nothing. The third is you reap what you sow. The fourth is that there are natural consequences for everything we do. The fifth is life is hard—get tough or die.

Of course, as a matter of kindness and charity, the landlord could, voluntarily and without force, exercise his freedom of choice to have compassion on Jake and let him stay in the apartment until he can get on his feet. An ideal scenario affords this as the best option—as long as Jake doesn't start to feel that it is his *right* to get something for nothing. Mandating charity would undermine the laws of nature and encourage a sense of entitlement. Therefore, yes, there is room for compassion. But it must come *voluntarily.* It can come from individuals; it can come from family; it can come from churches or charities. But it should not come from government. And it must never be mandated. Because when government starts passing laws mandating the action of particular values, those laws, no matter how well-meaning, start to collide with the laws of nature.

Matt and Money

Matt James grew up on a farm in the upper Midwest. He had a lot of firsthand experience with many of the laws of nature. Knowing the challenges of making a "good" living in agriculture, Matt's parents encouraged him and his siblings to get a good education and work toward successful, professional careers. This encouragement paid off: one of Matt's brothers is a doctor, one sister is a nurse, and another sister is a college professor. Matt himself got an MBA with an emphasis on finance and ultimately became a successful stockbroker in Chicago. He made a very good living and sought a lifestyle in keeping with his image and position to show off the fruits of his labors.

After a time, Matt grew weary of "keeping up with the Joneses," and, for the sake of his children and family, he quit. Matt James simply walked away from a successful career and a thriving brokerage and went back to the farm.

Matt had substantial savings and, for a time, things were easy. But eventually savings ran out, and for the first time Matt and his family experienced financial difficulty. In fact, they were flat broke, or at least, like many farmers, land rich and cash poor. For Matt and his family, it was a rude adjustment from their previous lifestyle. The financial challenges seemed to go on and on. At times they would get an influx of cash as crops came in or various other ventures experienced success, but inevitably it would go too quickly, leaving them out of money again. At one low point, Matt told his wife how he appreciated her for tightening the belt and working through it all as she had. "You have done so well with all of this," he said. "I appreciate the compliment," his wife replied, "but this whole thing is starting to feel a little bit like the story of the farmer who was trying to teach his horse to eat sawdust. Just when the horse finally started eating the sawdust, it starved to death and died. . . . I really don't know how much longer we can live on sawdust. How long are we going to have to keep doing this?"

Many of us have forgotten how to work with and manage our lives in accordance with the fundamental laws of nature. Instead of saving for a rainy day—or even next winter—we want it all now. Matt and his family, after years of living the "good life," had never learned to save and wait for the things they wanted. Old habits of living on credit were heavier to bear now that the farm afforded less predictability. Each time successes or windfalls came along, the income they brought in was gone as quickly as it had come.

Most of us recall the tale of the grasshopper and the ant: One summer day a grasshopper sang and chirped and hopped about, having a wonderful time. He met an ant who was busy gathering and storing grain for the winter. "Stop and talk with me," said the grasshopper. "We can sing and dance awhile." "Oh, no," said the ant. "Winter is coming and I must store up food. I think you should do the same." "Oh, I can't be bothered," the grasshopper replied. "Winter is a long time off and there is plenty of food." So the grasshopper continued to dance and sing, and the ant continued to work. When winter at last came, the grasshopper had no food and was starving. He went to the ant's house. "Can I have some wheat or maybe a few kernels of corn?" he asked. "Without it, I will starve." "You danced last summer," said the ant in disgust. "You can continue to dance." The ant gave him no food; he was left to fend for himself and get tough or die.

As financial winters came and went, Matt's family continued to struggle. They had to learn the lesson of the grasshopper. Matt understood that basic law of nature—get tough or die—well enough, and he set to work to turn things around. He began to realize that all he really needed to do was quit trying to get around the laws of nature, particularly as they apply to money and finance. He had to produce. He had to live within his means. It wasn't always easy and it took some time. Old habits die hard! But soon Matt took a whole new interest in self-sufficiency. He began to live the principles of producing what you consume, living within your means, and saving for a rainy day. Without credit and without debt, Matt and his family found themselves much better prepared for a wide range of possibilities that life might dish out and could live happier and without fear—as true assets to their family, friends, and community instead of liabilities.

Jake's First Banker

Let's read another story from Jake about legislated laws that enable and encourage violation of the laws of nature.

Jake enjoyed his new apartment and always paid his rent on time, but he was unsatisfied with life as a renter. After a time, by working two jobs, scrimping, saving, and even borrowing a little bit from his parents, Jake bought a dilapidated old motel and started remodeling the rooms into apartments. He did much of the work himself, and when the first apartment was finished, he moved in. Besides his full-time day job, he worked at a bakery, starting at 4:00 A.M. He left the bakery at 8:30 and went straight to his "regular" job until 5:00, and then he worked on the apartments when he got home in the afternoon, often until late at night. He was working hard, doing what people all over the world have always done to get ahead—putting his time, energy, and resources at risk, sowing seeds and planning to harvest the fruits of his labors. He avoided debt as much as possible, saving and paying as he went.

One evening a local banker came by to see what Jake was up to. Impressed, the banker told Jake, "When you get two of these units finished, let me know. I want to come have a look at them." When Jake got two units finished, he went to see the banker, who offered Jake a loan. He offered Jake the resources necessary to finish the other units quickly, get them rented, and start earning an income on his project.

When they sat down to discuss the project, the banker explained, "My job as a banker is easy as long as three simple rules are followed: 1) I'm dealing with honest people who have some integrity; 2) They have genuine 'skin in the game'—something at risk—based on a significant down payment or equity or hard work; and 3) They have the ability to manage the asset, improve it, and increase its value. With those three things in place, I never have a problem. Sometimes I can get by with just two of the three, but if I violate or bend those rules, then I inevitably start having problems."

No wonder we're in a banking crisis in this country! Jake got his loan. He continued to work hard and made good on his banker's investment. The banker did well by following rules based on the commonsense, economic laws of nature. But many bankers in this country have been ignoring the laws of nature for years, giving loans to borrowers who didn't verify income, who had no "skin in the game" and nothing at risk. For years, virtually all anyone had to do to get a loan was have a pulse. Any warm body could get a loan or a credit card. A responsible track record wasn't necessary. What could bankers expect to happen? Well, expected or not, it happened.

The federal government played a big role in this irresponsibility. Even worse, once it didn't work, what has the government done about it? Ignoring basic laws of nature and without addressing real causes, the federal government has been rushing around trying to pass laws to put Band-Aids on symptoms. Not only is Congress passing a whole bevy of laws, but also the quasi-government mortgage giants and federal banking regulators have adopted a whole slew of new rules and regulations that are essentially meaningless—restrictions, for example, that prohibit any change to the terms of a loan within seven days of buying a home or prohibit the resale of any property within ninety days of closing. These policies are not where the problem lies. If government and the bankers would simply get back to basics—those simple principles stated by Jake's banker and based on the laws of nature—the market would quickly sort itself out.

Pearl's Story

Sound banking principles make sound banks. Not only do they provide for the integrity and ability to pay, as with Jake, but also the desire and willingness to stick it out, such as with Pearl Williams. For years prior to the 1970s, a down payment on a mortgage was typically 20 percent. Why? Because requiring a sizeable investment is the "skin in the game" that Jake's banker talked about. People work harder to protect that which they have worked hard to get. Pearl's story is a good case in point.

Pearl is a victim of timing. A school teacher in Florida, Pearl and her husband got into a nice, comfortable home when they moved there almost twenty years ago. They had a beautiful daughter named Ebony, and life was good. But life doesn't always go as planned, and after more than a decade in Florida, Pearl found herself a divorced, single mother. Although she and her husband had earned a good deal of equity in their home, the market had appreciated enough that when they got divorced, neither could afford to keep the house. So Pearl took her equity and invested in a townhouse where she and her daughter lived happily for the next five years until Ebony was a junior in high school.

A cheerleader, homecoming queen, and class favorite, Ebony was a popular teenager. Pearl was very proud of her daughter, and over time she started to feel that their otherwise adequate townhouse was inadequate in terms of the social status she wanted to portray for her. She started thinking about buying a new home and set her sights on a 1,800-square-foot home priced close to $340,000. Although Pearl herself had grown up alongside four siblings in a 1,200-square-foot home, the larger home for just herself and her daughter was still considered modest by today's standards and seemed more appropriate for the image Pearl hoped to portray. Besides, she had a good job and more than $120,000 equity in the townhouse, so she thought she ought to be able to swing it—and why shouldn't she? A house is a good investment, right? By now it was autumn 2006.

Pearl found credit easy to come by. With her large down payment, it wasn't hard to qualify for a mortgage. She bought the new house using the equity in her townhouse as a sizeable (more than 35 percent) down payment. When Pearl and Ebony moved into their home, the carpet still smelled new. They had dozens of neighbors as new to the neighborhood as they were, and as the development filled up, lawns greened and new trees bloomed. It was postcard-perfect suburban America. But it was all too easy. Most of her neighbors didn't have the kind of down payment that Pearl had; most had put down 5 percent or less. Today, those neighbors are all gone.

When the market crumbled and their home values and paper equity collapsed, they walked. Now, with Ebony off at college, Pearl lives in her house alone. In fact, she is virtually the only person left in the entire subdivision, as dozens of homes have been abandoned, leaving the once up-and-coming neighborhood a virtual ghost town. The value of her house has fallen to less than $150,000, but Pearl hangs on because she's got real "skin in the game." Unlike her neighbors who vacated their homes, she has more than fifteen years' worth of hard-earned equity tied up in her house, and she's willing to hang on to see if it will come back. Luckily for her bank, it has at least one borrower who qualified under at least two of the three principles. Too bad for Pearl the banks that loaned on the houses around her didn't follow the same tried-and-true rules of banking.

Gravity—Or, Water Always Runs Downhill

Gravity is one of nature's easiest laws to understand. We can't see gravity, but we don't doubt its existence. We see and feel its effects continually. And, as with all laws of nature, there is no getting around it. If all the nations in the whole world got together and passed a law stating that there was no more gravity, nature wouldn't listen or obey—there would still be gravity. And it would still do what it does regardless of the laws or opinions of man.

Our third commonsense rule of banking asserts that a potential borrower needs a demonstrated track record of being able to add value or improve assets. Until 2006, even borrowers with a recent bankruptcy could get a loan. Many amateur investors were buying and selling—*flipping*—houses and properties for a profit. They say when your hair dresser, carpet guy, insurance agent, butcher, and cousin are all doing something they know nothing about, you'd better stay out of it because there is going to be a problem. House flipping is a pretty good example of that.

Gravity makes water run downhill. At times we start to think that we can change the effects of gravity by building a dam or rerouting a river. We might even congratulate ourselves on our brief success. But eventually, gravity always wins. If we build a dam and stop the flow of water, it works for a time. But after the resulting reservoir fills, we either have to release the water or it begins to run over the top. In the end, water always runs downhill; in the end, gravity always wins.

The mortgage craze—the fast paced, overinflated buying and selling; the loose and easy loans; the *flipping*—was like defying gravity. In the end, it just can't work. It's only a matter of time. In the end, water always runs downhill.

Other Examples

During the dot-com run, it was common to hear, "it's a new economy," or "the old rules don't apply." "You don't need to actually produce something to generate income and produce profit," we were told. "You don't need a good profit/earnings ratio in a company in order for it to be a good investment." We were actually hearing that companies don't need to be profitable! "Buy now or you'll miss out" was the message. And it sucked a lot of us in, even though we knew it didn't make sense. Our friend Worth Woolsey is a little bit old school. He likes to say, "If it sounds too good to be true, you can bet your lucky stars it is."

It seems those old-schoolers know what they're talking about. Maybe they know something we don't. Or maybe they just haven't forgotten the laws of nature.

Fear and greed normally keep each other in check. But in the dot-com frenzy many people let fear and greed run together and tip the scales of logic. "Buy now or miss out" started sounding reasonable despite all the red flags. Instead of feeling a healthy fear of loss ("What if this asset can't pay as advertised?"), we believed we had better rush to get on board or the train would leave without us. This frantic rush to get involved without solid data, against sound investment principles, did not work out for the shareholders of thousands of dot-com companies. The rabid trend of overselling, of flying in the face of good economic practices—like the mortgage craze—could not hold back gravity. In the end, it simply could not work.

What about our banker's three rules? How did we, as a country, build a sand dam in the banking/real estate world and violate the principles that work with the natural laws of economics and finance? Remember principle number one: only lend money to those who are honest. One recent trend saw "stated income loans"—otherwise now known as a "liar loans"—become common. These were loans where the buyer could claim he made X amount of dollars, but he didn't have to verify his income. For years, bankers followed a simple rule of "trust but verify," but without that practice in place, many people overstated their income and bought homes they could not afford. Some realtors and banks simply penciled in the required numbers. Where do you think that ended up leaving the bankers?

What Have We Learned?

As we endure the worst recession and greatest economic downturn since the Great Depression, we have actually done little, if anything, to return to the laws of nature. Congress continues to "add sand to the top of the dam," but as with all such situations, it's only a matter of time; the water must be released somewhere. If we don't stop ignoring the laws of nature that govern economics and finance, this dam will not only overflow, but there is also a good chance that it will build up enough pressure to completely collapse. And who knows what the resulting flood will wash away? Natural laws always eventually become self-evident. Water must eventually flow. Finance will eventually follow its commonsense laws or self-destruct. And, just like Pearl, many who built well out of the flood plain, who invested well in the safe zone, will get destroyed when the dam collapses and causes a tidal wave of financial destruction. For some recovering federalists these are major acknowledgments.

Mancos and "Easy" Credit

This is another story about Mancos. Like Matt James, Mancos has agricultural roots. As a youngster, Mancos grew up on a horse, roaming backfields and exploring canyons. Upon retirement, he naturally gravitated back to his roots and bought a small ranch with horses and livestock to serve as a gathering place for his family. During the era of easy credit, Mancos was busy improving his ranch. He was offered easy financing on building materials and a design package—no interest, no payments for a year. How could he pass it up? No interest! He could take the money he would otherwise pay for the materials, put it in a safe, secure CD, and come out money ahead. It was a no-brainer.

Then things began to go wrong. First there were major defects with the materials. Mancos had an inherent tendency to forget the old adage "you get what you pay for," but when he sought recourse with the merchant, he found the merchant in financial trouble and unable to make it right.

Mancos didn't think it was right that he should get stuck having to pay twice, first for the materials and then again to replace them. He took hope in the terms of the "easy financing" contract, which provided recourse for defective products and services against both the merchant and the creditor, and he sought accountability and recourse through the creditor. Long before the first payment was due, he sent a letter to the creditor explaining the problem and seeking resolution. The creditor ignored him. He sent a second letter and still got no response. A third letter was also ignored. Finally, long after the one-year-no-payment/no-interest period was over, the creditor responded to inform him that the dispute had been resolved in the merchant's favor, and the original principal balance was due plus back interest at a high percentage rate for the entire previous year.

Mancos was incensed. He protested the action and considered filing suit against both the creditor and the merchant, but he had come to detest litigation. In fact, he had become so jaded with the justice system that he couldn't bring himself to do it. Instead, he offered to deposit the entire amount in dispute into an escrow account pending a legitimate dispute-resolution process.

The company ignored his offer, so he refused to make any payments in hopes of getting their attention. Throughout the next year Mancos sent multiple letters and spent hours on the telephone, often frustrated and often talking to a foreign call-center agent who was difficult to understand and knew nothing about his situation. In the end, Mancos had no choice but to file a lawsuit to try to straighten out the mess, including the resulting damage to his credit rating, all for the sake of some "easy financing."

Application of the Laws of Nature to Property Rights

The laws of nature can be applied to virtually every situation, including controversial social/political issues. Although we're not going to get into such controversial social issues as part of this discussion, many of us—the authors collectively writing as Publius MMX—are deeply rooted in real estate. We come from all over the country, but whether we live in a high-rise or a ranch house, one thing many of us have in common is a strong love for the land. Consequently, property rights tend to be a pet subject for us.

Human beings naturally acquire private ownership of various forms of property when they put their own time, energy, and resources at risk to acquire such property and put it to beneficial use. Such private ownership has a natural effect on what people do and how they view property. Somehow property becomes more personal, meaningful, and significant when ownership is assigned. It has always been this way. When Fred Flintstone and Barney Rubble struck two stones together and, through their time and efforts, were able to fashion arrowheads, those arrowheads were theirs until they lost possession of them, whether by use, theft, or sale.

There was no law stating that the arrowheads belonged to Fred. There didn't need to be. They belonged to him because he put his time, energy, and resources at risk to improve and add value to the raw stones and put them to beneficial use. In the process he naturally acquired private ownership—property rights—to that arrowhead. Remember the Little Red Hen?

Mancos and the Surplus Liquid Oxygen Tank—Use It or Lose It—Possession Is Nine-tenths of the Law

In terms of fundamental property rights, Mancos has another story. In his regular travels across a local Indian reservation, Mancos noticed a large, white, liquid oxygen tank with a posted "for sale" sign. He thought of what a good water storage tank it might make for one of the livestock wells on his ranch and called the number. The tank belonged to the Indian tribe that occupied the reservation where it was located. They had acquired it as "surplus" from the federal government and had later determined that they didn't need it, so it was for sale. That seemed easy enough, so Mancos quickly wrote a check and received a bill of sale proving it was his.

Buying the tank was the easy part; the problem was moving the thing. The 7,500-gallon, double-layered, insulated, liquid oxygen tank was very big and heavy, and awkward to move. And it was going to require all kinds of special permits. Mancos explored various possibilities for moving it, but nothing fell together right away. Time passed, and he eventually bought another smaller water tank that was easier to move and set it up at the well. He still wanted the liquid oxygen tank for additional storage but still couldn't get it moved. More time passed; Mancos received offers to buy the tank. He decided to hang onto it, but he still had not solved the dilemma of how to move it, and more time passed.

Then one day Mancos noticed that the tank was gone! Just disappeared! Mancos saw red. What had happened to his tank, the tank he had paid for, the tank he had a bill of sale for? He headed straight for the tribal office. It turns out that someone else had wanted to buy the tank, and since Mancos had never moved it and taken possession of it, they sold it to the new party, who did move it. Mancos was livid. He had a bill of sale—not with him but somewhere—but he could get no information about where the tank had gone.

On his way home, Mancos started to cool off. He even started to chuckle at the situation. It had been five years. He had possession of a piece of paper, a bill of sale, that said the tank was his. But after five years he still had never taken possession of the tank and moved it. As Mancos laughed at himself, he realized that he really had no one to blame but himself. He acknowledged the irrefutable reality that when we do nothing, nature takes its course. When it comes to property rights, according to the laws of nature, eventually it boils down to *use it or lose it*—resources will eventually be put to beneficial use by someone. Mancos acknowledged that despite his bill of sale and all the laws that might be on the books, in the end, none of that could trump the irrefutable reality that possession is nine-tenths of the law. In the end, nature takes its course.

Application to Land—Otherwise Known as Real Property

Although it gets more complex with real property—land—the same concepts apply. When settlers first ventured into the wilderness to put their time, energy, and resources at risk to claim and tame raw land, clearing it, planting it, and putting it to beneficial use, it became theirs. Regardless of law or deed, it was theirs as long as they could defend and maintain possession of it. Such property rights were not created by any law of man; they existed naturally from the outset. These rights were basic, fundamental, inalienable rights naturally endowed by the laws of nature and of nature's God.

Fast-forward a few centuries. Today most zoning and land use ordinances disregard the concept of natural law and inalienable property rights. In accordance with the principles of the laws of nature, any appropriate land use ordinance should start out by saying that, as a matter of natural law, private property ownership entitles a person freedom to choose what to do with the property so far as it does not infringe upon the rights of others.

Instead, what we see are cookie-cutter, one-size-fits-all land use ordinances that essentially state, "You have no right to do anything whatsoever with your property except that which this ordinance specifically grants. And any use not specifically granted is specifically prohibited!"

These ordinances typically grant government complete control over any and all land uses. Even if a use is specifically listed as a "permitted" use, actually engaging in that use often requires a specific permit, which means that rather than simply looking at the list, seeing that your intended use is permitted, and going ahead with it, you are usually required by such ordinances to go to the applicable building or land-use department, pay an application or permit fee, and acquire specific permission in order to do what the ordinance already says you are entitled to do. If you fail to pay applicable fees, jump through the hoops, and get the required permit(s), such ordinances typically provide that your use or project can be shut down, and you can be fined for attempting to do anything on your property without the required permit(s). These requirements can even apply to such simple things as installing a new furnace or changing a water heater.

Such ordinances may list a number of permitted uses but not specifically include such things as "swing set," "jungle gym," or "solar panel," which means that they are all prohibited. Under such ordinances, there are generally only two ways around this: 1) you can request a special "conditional use" permit, in which case a number of additional conditions can be placed on the permit, including getting the blessing from all your neighbors, or 2) you can try to get the ordinance amended to specifically authorize such uses as "permitted uses." In either case, it's bound to be a long, slow bureaucratic trudge, rife with red tape and frustration—all to get government permission to do what you are already naturally and inherently entitled to do with your own private property.

What all such laws and ordinances are saying is that they—manmade laws—are now the *source* of property rights and entitlements without any recognition of the preexisting and inalienable rights of all men that existed long before governments even existed and before infringing governmental regulations were even dreamt of! These laws are inconsistent with the fundamental laws of nature and violate inalienable property rights and freedom of choice.

Contrary to the laws of nature, state and national leagues and associations of cities, towns, and municipalities, as well as other city and state associations, often encourage and enable local governments to take private property rights through ordinances that fail to recognize inherent, inalienable rights. Such governmental attempts to usurp natural property rights are wrong! Copious land use ordinances and dictatorial property laws don't work. Basic property rights don't come from man or man-made law. The right to own and improve property according to our own will and ability is a fundamental tenet of the laws of nature and a basic concept that needs to be clearly understood.

Cause and Effect Relationship of Private Property Ownership

Property ownership has a profound effect on the human psyche. When we claim ownership of a thing, we have a natural tendency to take pride in it, to care for it, improve it, and add value to it. We are organically inspired to increase and refine that which is ours. Remember the effect true ownership had in Pearl's neighborhood? The fact that she had truly worked to acquire her home—had "real skin in the game"—instilled in her a unique pride and willingness to endure far beyond that of her neighbors.

And what about defense? How much effort are people going to put into defending property that doesn't even belong to them? How far are they going to stick their necks out? To what extent are people going to voluntarily put their lives on the line to defend and protect property they don't own? The natural psychological effects of private property ownership are well-established.

This phenomenon has been demonstrated in countless ways throughout history. It is not a well-known fact that when our Pilgrim forebears came to this land, they first attempted to hold all things in common, without private property ownership. This proved unsuccessful. In common ownership they could not produce enough to feed themselves, and, if not for the help of their American-Indian neighbors, they would have starved. But once they assigned private property ownership, pride *and productivity* increased, providing more abundant harvests and a more enterprising, successful community.

This same principle was well-proven in the former Soviet Union. On a proportionate basis, Soviet citizens could, and did, produce more food in their own backyards than they did on the large, collective farms. In fact, in communist Cuba this principle and private "backyard" production essentially saved the country from mass starvation during the period following the collapse of the Soviet Union, which discontinued massive shipments of grain and other staples from the former Soviet Union to Cuba. Unbeknown to most Americans, this lack of Soviet food shipments, combined with the U.S. embargo, seriously tested the ability of Cuba and its collective farms to feed the country. Although the collective farms—like the collective farms in the Soviet Union and our own Pilgrim forefathers' collective efforts—failed that test, the Cuban people, with private ownership and production from their backyard gardens, stepped up to the plate and produced enough food to avert the crisis. These examples are testaments to the importance of fundamental property rights and the cause-and-effect relationship of private property ownership.

Issues with the Laws of Nature

One of the biggest issues many of us have with the laws of nature is that we don't want to wait for nature to take its course! We live in a world of instant gratification. We have gotten into the bad habit of wanting everything yesterday. We don't want to wait for markets to correct themselves any more than we want to wait for the car, furniture, home, toy or high-tech gadget that we can't yet afford. Again, this is true individually and collectively. Our governments are as guilty of this buy-now, pay-later mentality as anyone, and our governments have done much to foster and perpetuate this thinking. On the other hand, our governmental policies also reflect our values as a people.

But when nature can and does move more quickly than we anticipate, we expect government to step in and take primary responsibility for cleaning up the mess. It can sometimes seem that government has become so powerful in our sight that we no longer believe it is subject to the laws of nature. Governments themselves often behave as though they have the ability to circumvent the laws of nature. Consequently, we want—we expect—big government to keep us safe, to solve our problems, to pay our debts. We have come to expect government to be the umbrella that protects us from life. We don't want the responsibility; we prefer a safety net. We don't want to save up and pay as we go; we don't want to work for what we have; we don't want to solve our own dilemmas. We want to have someone tell us exactly what we can and can't do. And we want to have it all now, pay later, and blame someone else. And thank heaven, of course there are exceptions to every rule.

Somewhere along the way we have picked up the idea that when we allow people to experience the consequences of their actions, we're punishing them. In reality, we cripple people when we interfere with the laws of nature and don't allow them to experience the natural consequences of their decisions and actions. Jake's uncle once told him, after Jake commiserated about a mistake he had made that had cost him thousands of dollars, "An education costs no matter how you get it." Jake's dad followed up by saying, "Learn from your mistakes quickly so that you can get on with making up for them!"

No one can provide a safety net or a bubble of protection forever. Eventually we all must step out on our own and learn from our mistakes in order to experience the growth and satisfaction that go along with navigating our own solutions. As our friend Worth likes to say, "Everything in life has its cost, and eventually someone will pay." It is wrong to shield people from the natural consequences of their decisions and actions and deprive them of the opportunity to learn. In nature, he who thrives is he who learns.

Chapter 6

What Happens When the Actions (and Laws) of Men Collide with the Laws of Nature?

Many of us have heard the story about the aircraft carrier caught in the fog. As the carrier was cruising along, it received an urgent radio transmission:

> Please divert your course 15 degrees north to avoid collision.
>
> The carrier responded: Recommend you divert YOUR course 15 degrees south to avoid collision.
>
> Reply: No; I say again, divert your course.
>
> Carrier: This is the captain of a U.S. Navy ship. Repeat, divert YOUR course.
>
> Reply: Divert immediately to avoid collision.
>
> Carrier: THIS IS THE AIRCRAFT CARRIER USS ABRAHAM LINCOLN, THE SECOND LARGEST SHIP IN THE ATLANTIC FLEET. WE ARE ACCOMPANIED BY THREE DESTROYERS, THREE CRUISERS, AND NUMEROUS SUPPORT VESSELS. I DEMAND THAT YOU CHANGE YOUR COURSE, OR COUNTERMEASURES WILL BE TAKEN TO ENSURE THE SAFTEY OF THIS SHIP.
>
> Reply: Fine. This is a lighthouse. Your call.

Just as the lighthouse high on a rocky outcropping is immovable and uncompromising, so are the laws of nature unyielding when it comes to natural cause and effect. We cannot avoid them, however much we would like to do so. Our country and our government are on a collision course with the immovable laws of nature. It does not matter how we protest or how we plan or scheme. It does not matter if our opinion is opposed to this. The lighthouse won't move; the rocks won't dissolve. Just like cruising an early spring ice field aboard the Titanic, the best and greatest laws of men will fail and sink when they collide with the laws of nature. It will not matter if the collision does not seem very hard; when we collide with nature we cannot win. As one of this country's most revered writers has said, "Whether we and our politicians know it or not, Nature is party to all our deals and decisions, and she has more votes, a longer memory, and a sterner sense of justice than we do." In any conflict between man-made forces and the forces of nature—including a conflict of laws—nature wins every time.

One Last Story about the Sinking of a Community Bank

Great titans of the banking industry have violated the laws of nature. By now, some of these giants have either collapsed in a cloud of dust or were deemed "too big to fail" and were bailed out with government funds. What about community banks? What about smaller, local bankers who don't follow the basic rules of Jake's first banker? What happens to them when they collide with the laws of nature?

In the case we're going to tell you about, the first inkling of trouble came in a letter to bank shareholders. According to the story, a letter, signed by the CEO of the bank, stated that the board of directors had approved a dividend of thirty cents per share for the first six months of the year. The news sent nervous shivers through many of the shareholders; payments in June and November of the preceding year amounted to $3.85 per share—the biggest annual dividend ever paid by the bank, then in its 127th year. At that time, said the CEO, the bank had had a very good year. This time, though, the ground was shifting, and the CEO and his board of directors were not so pleased. Late in 2007, the real estate bubble that had lifted the bank to record profits had started to sag.

As it turned out, that thirty-cent dividend was to be the last payment shareholders would ever receive from the bank. The run of profitable years making loans to land developers and builders had ground to a halt.

The bank was entering a nightmare period of losses and crumbling capital reserves that the CEO and his directors would prove powerless to stop.

The ordeal would continue for about eighteen months until regulators, certain there was no hope for the dying institution, confiscated the bank, wiping out shareholders and staining the reputations of the bank managers and top executives. The closure set off a surge of accusations and recriminations among an inner circle of influential shareholders and bank managers that continues unabated today.

"Five years ago, this bank was considered one of the best community banks in the country," said an investment banker who joined the board of directors late in the game. "It had a great franchise. But somewhere in the last five years, the board of directors started making very risky decisions." By the time he came on board, the bank was already in serious trouble.

One shareholder still doesn't know why the bank died or who is responsible, but the sixty-two-year-old widow feels suddenly vulnerable. The financial cushion bequeathed to her by her late husband is gone. "All I know is the bank has squandered my inheritance. It was what I considered to be my future security to get me over the rough edges of retirement," she said.

"Blaming the economy is an easy out," wrote one blogger, whose great-great-great-grandfather helped found the bank in 1881. "I believe it was mismanagement, exuberance, nepotism, and opaque communications from the board of directors. Our family lost a lot of money. But the most wrenching part is the feeling that we lost a legacy."

Construction and real estate development had always been solid in the bank's home state. Historically, real estate loans didn't seem hazardous. As recently as 2007, losses on real estate-secured loans amounted to less than 1 percent of the bank's loan portfolio. Consequently, according to the CFO, "I don't think there were any decisions made that seemed like high-risk or wrong decisions at the time."

Instead, the CFO blamed shareholders who he claimed engaged in inflammatory actions that scared other shareholders, frightened depositors, and touched off a $100 million run on deposits, claiming that this probably forced regulators to close the bank prematurely, when it could possibly have been saved.

"I don't think these shareholders really understood the impact of what they were doing," the CFO said, adding that the media shared the blame for printing leading reports that fueled the bank run.

A letter sent from shareholders to other shareholders called for a meeting with bank management to discuss, among other things, a document formally acknowledging an agreement between the Federal Reserve and the bank, and commanding the bank to increase its capital reserves, which had been decimated by construction and land development loans that had gone bad during the previous two years. The shareholders saw this document as a formal acknowledgment that the bank was in trouble despite its long history of solidarity.

The situation was precarious, but the CFO had not been alarmed. The bank had a troubling $32 million in loan losses during 2008 but had set aside more than $100 million to cover them, he said. The bank had also been working to comply with corrective measures suggested unofficially by regulators during previous meetings. He was surprised when the Fed issued a written statement formally instructing the bank to present an acceptable plan to increase its capital within 60 days. The Fed didn't say what might happen if the bank failed to comply, but the message was clear: regulators were worried.

"I thought we were doing what was requested and were following good procedure," the CFO said. "I didn't feel like the bank was under any more stress than other banks in the same markets."

What the CFO didn't know was that another federal agency, the Federal Deposit Insurance Corp. (FDIC), had secretly put the bank on its closely watched "problems list" a month earlier. The list contained the names of more than three hundred lenders, its highest level since 1994, testifying to the gravity of the current U.S. financial crisis. "That's not something they communicated to the bank," the CFO said.

Turmoil inside the bank mounted over the next few months. Loans continued to sour, and by fall 2009 the bank was showing losses of more than $200 million. Shareholders were becoming uneasy. While bank managers tried to paint a picture of security, the bank had not paid a dividend in over a year. Then came the shareholder letter, stating that it was likely that the Fed would issue a "prompt corrective action" letter at any time.

"Letters of this type," wrote the alarmed shareholder, "are written to banks that have engaged in such egregious practices for so long that the regulators deem the [FDIC] insurance fund better protected from losses than by a continuation of the same management and director team." According to the shareholder letter, it was unlikely regulators would give the bank much more time to turn the bank around because of "management's continued lack of response over the past year and a half."

The FDIC letter arrived two weeks later, stating the bank was "critically undercapitalized." It ordered the bank to find a suitable buyer or raise enough capital by a stated deadline. Although the consequences were not spelled out, the implication was clear: failure to comply would mean the end of the bank.

Then another shareholder wrote another letter. "Time is short," it said. Share prices had plunged from $150 to less than $5 a share in less than ten months. "Bank managers have made it clear that they do not accept any responsibility for this decline," the letter said.

According to the CFO, the bank needed at least $50 million and as much as $100 million in new capital to stave off regulators. But raising capital in such a heated environment was nearly impossible. Over the course of the next 30 days, depositors withdrew nearly $100 million from the bank. The writing was on the wall; the bank was collapsing.

Shareholders claim that bank executives have no one to blame but themselves. Instead of blaming shareholder letters or media hype, according to them, executives should have acknowledged three key mistakes that ultimately doomed the bank: 1) instead of diversifying its loans, the bank focused on construction and land development; 2) it also expanded into fast-growing real estate markets, making loans to unknown, unfamiliar builders and developers; and 3) it relied too much on brokered deposits—funds raised by brokers from investors around the country chasing high interest rates—instead of relying on local depositors who would be more loyal to the bank.

The conclusion, according to the new investment banker on the board of directors: "Any blip will sink a bank situated this way faster than a comparable community bank because they have a much higher-risk profile." This one cost the FDIC deposit insurance fund almost $300 million.

This is what happens when ships collide with rocky outcroppings. What happens when bad sense collides with the laws of nature—laws that should provide the fundamental measuring stick for evaluating everything we do, from personal choices to business and government? What should be the relationship between these fundamental laws of nature and the laws of men? Yet there are many examples of fundamental conflict between the laws of nature and the laws and actions of our nation. When the laws and actions of man are in conflict with the laws of nature, what is ultimately going to happen? Although this is the story of a community bank, it describes the same basic path—the same course—our country is on and should be a sobering reality check. On the other hand, there is no question, America is considered to be "too big to fail." But that statement raises a few questions. Top on that list is: *Since when should the United States of America need to be bailed out by anyone?* Moreover, who is big enough to bail us out? And, finally, what will be the consequences if they do?

Chapter 7

What Is the Destiny of America on Its Present Course?

If America stays on its present track, what will our future look like? The kids are already asking, "Are we there yet?" And the reality is, in terms of what it will look like if we stay on the present course, we're almost there—it's almost in sight.

Just for the sake of discussion, let's assume that the aircraft carrier we talked about earlier is now a monstrous cruise ship—our great American ship of state, the USS United States—and we're all spectators on this great American dream cruise. We're taking a big cruise around the world. We're all along for the ride, having a great time, and enjoying all the nice scenery.

The reality is, for at least the last tweny years America has been on the functional equivalent of a party cruise, with thrilling entertainment and rich buffets. In our highs, we have allowed indifference to take the wheel. Somewhere along the way, our vessel became the USS United States of Entertainment. We have handed over the controls to bandits and gone to sleep with our tummies full, our appetites satiated, and our heads clouded. Is it too late to steer clear of trouble?

If it were our cruise ship, instead of the aircraft carrier, moving through the fog, bearing down on the rocks, where could we turn? If we were able to heed the lighthouse and managed to correct course abruptly enough to avoid the imminent, rocky cliffs, could we still make it back to sunnier waters? Could we make it back to our golden state of living, to our land of milk and honey? And what does the promised land look like at this point?

California, America's own Golden State, was once a Mecca for Americans seeking a more successful lifestyle. It was the epitome of the

American dream. But how has that turned out? How has that dream survived our time away, while we've been on our dream cruise? Has prosperity been good to the land of sunshine, or was it wasted? With a state debt of more than $500 billion and an unemployment debt alone of $7.5 billion, a place that was once an icon for productivity and prosperity is now a poster child for mismanagement and overspending.

After all the borrowing and spending, after all the taxation and regulatory chokeholds on business and free enterprise, after throwing "living within our means" to the wind—consuming far more than it produces and ignoring good common sense, ignoring so many of the laws of nature for so long, and living like there was no tomorrow—California is struggling to stay afloat. Businesses are leaving in droves. Agriculture has no water. Family farms are virtually gone. Production has moved offshore. Even technology and innovation, once California's apex, have dwindled. With revenue down in so many areas, California is in real trouble.

But California is hardly alone. Arizona, New York, and Illinois are close behind in terms of failed state financial management. An array of monopolies, government policies, severe overspending, and unjust business practices have combined to make what were previously some of the most prosperous states in our country vulnerable and leave them in sharp decline. And the list of states in real danger of bankruptcy is only growing longer.

Agriculture, one of California's foundational mainstays for generations, is an ideal example and representation of poor management and the big-government takeover of prosperous productive pursuits. California was once the core of America's fruit and vegetable supply, but now most of the small agricultural operations are gone. Long-standing collusions between government and big business have sucked the lifeblood from the industry. Federal subsidies go to giant, corporate producers, making it virtually impossible for smaller family farms to compete. In turn, giant conglomerates absorb family agriculture at an ever-increasing pace. Crop diversity has declined, and genetically modified crops increase corporate control of the American food supply.

Let us not forget that agriculture and the soil are often said to be the foundation of civilization. While fewer and fewer people in this country really seem to think or care much about agriculture per se, it still represents and reflects the most basic concept of *production.* Civilized societies and sustainable economies are based on production. During the American Revolutionary era, the vast majority of people lived or worked on farms. Agricultural production was the productive backbone of this country and spawned a series of westward migrations in America in pursuit of Manifest Destiny, based on the potential for a corresponding increase in agricultural production and national prosperity. The promise of rich, fertile soil in the Willamette Valley is what built the Oregon Trail. And second only to the fleeting allure of gold, rich, fertile soil was likewise the biggest early attraction to California. As recently as the WWII era, a majority of Americans still lived and worked on farms and actively produced. Today, only a small percentage of Americans work the soil or have any real connection to it.

Again, for purposes of this discussion, agriculture is simply being used as an example—albeit a very obvious one—of what is happening essentially across the board in this country. Although we are becoming increasingly dependent upon foreign agricultural imports, and the number of agricultural producers in this country has steadily deceased to the point that the number is now about 1 percent of our total population, the number of government agencies, administrators, employees, bureaucrats, laws, rules, and regulations that govern those few producers has increased steadily. Without even getting into such questions as what modern agricultural practices are doing to our soil—*the foundation of our civilization*—the real question here is where is "civilization" headed as we depart from its productive foundation? As society has changed, what do we have to show for it? What are we producing now?

As food giants prosper, they often decide they can reduce production costs even further by moving to places like Brazil. Since they already own and control so much of the land and resources in California and elsewhere, to maintain an iron grip and monopoly on the market, they participate in further collusion to restrict the water supply or sell their water for other uses to places like Las Vegas and let the ground lie fallow. In fact, the collusion is so strong that government even *pays* them *not* to produce by fallowing the ground. The net effect is that we are now heavily dependent on imported food, not to mention energy. It seems like we've got all kinds of problems, but let us not forget the old Chinese proverb: lots of food, lots of problems; no food, one problem.

But unless we live there, who cares about California, right? California is California's problem. Who cares about agriculture, energy, and technology? We can get our food from Mexico and Brazil, our petroleum from Canada and Saudi Arabia, and our technology from Asia.

Hollywood: now that's the California that really matters. But so they say, "As goes California, so goes the nation." The federal government has been propping up California for a long time. Maybe what is happening in California is a harbinger we should all fear.

At the end of February 2010, thirty states had borrowed more than $33 billion dollars from the federal government at 5 percent interest. But this debt doesn't show in the state budgets because it will be paid for via a direct tax to employers, further damping the opportunity for recovery and growth.

Eventually, based on precedent with AIG and the U.S. auto industry, all of which were "too big to fail," California, New York, Illinois, and others are likewise going to be deemed too big to fail, and the financial load will then be added to the backs of taxpayers everywhere via federal government bailouts in our "all for one and one for all" federal financial scheme. And, as with the auto industry and AIG, the federal government will then own a controlling stake in these states and, just as it manages its current controlling stakes in the so-called private sector, it will likewise dictate how the states operate.

We have been traveling the road to federal takeover of the states for a long time. Current stimulus packages demonstrate an obvious and intentional fleecing of private sector capital via government injections into the public sector, where elite and sometimes unsuspecting, professional politicians make deals based on keeping their friends and contributors happy; elected state and local officials have little, if any, influence, as prior agreements with the power parties and the federal government set a pace that gives newly elected figures no sway; and corporate/public partnerships make the bulk of the decisions that citizen legislators and local government executives used to make.

In further continuance of this accelerating trend, the federal government continues to grow, becoming the biggest organization, biggest employer, and most powerful entity in the country. We may already be there. A *Wall Street Journal* article in February 2010 titled "The Public-Union Ascendancy" states that in 2009, the number of unionized workers who work for the government surpassed those in the private economy for the first time. In 2008, the number of government employees surpassed the number of employees in manufacturing and construction. The more the numbers grow, the more dependent we become. With federal control over our paychecks, our media, and our rights, there is little independence left, and states become mere cogs in the wheel of a gigantic, powerful, federal machine.

And the thing we need to remember about all these federal and other government jobs is that aside from paychecks, *they produce no tangible, marketable products; they produce nothing of value!* While such jobs may produce a paycheck and other plush benefits, which may be "assets" to the people who receive them, there is a corresponding liability for everyone else who has to pay the bill without any corresponding production or generation of marketable goods or services that can contribute positively to the American GDP. In other words, at this point and increasingly, as a nation, we are burning equity much faster than we are adding value to produce and build it, with no corresponding production or return, or even reasonable hope of corresponding return. Remember Jake's banker's three basic rules for lending, especially the third one? As a borrower, what is the federal government doing to improve or add value to its assets? Under such circumstances, based on the irrefutable laws of nature that apply to economics, the farther we head down this path, unless we change course, inevitably, at some point, this path turns into a dead end—which is fine as long as we are going to be happy and satisfied with what we find at the end of that path.

In the mean time, what happens to states like Washington, Virginia, Utah, and others that have done a better job of managing their resources, adhering to the laws of nature, staying afloat, maintaining some semblance of independence, and resisting further encroachment by the federal government? We hate to break the news, but on the present track it's only a matter of time for them too, as the federal government will ask their taxpayers, along with everyone else, to share in the burden of the failing states' debt. And this particular discussion does not even mention or take into account the massive federal spending and debt that we already share, which will be discussed in more detail in our next essays.

Our destination, on the present course, is coming into sight. The party cruise is coming to an end, and we're about to wake up with a hangover! In short, the future looks pretty bleak. At this point, we could engage in all kinds of speculation about what variations of worst-case or even likely-case scenarios will ultimately occur if the United States stays on its present course. But we'll leave that to other doom and gloomers—heaven knows, there's no shortage. We don't have a crystal ball, and it is fair to say that none of us knows exactly what is going to happen. Although most of us know in our guts that we've been in very troubled waters and our easy ride is near its end, a message of doom and gloom is not the most important message we need to hear at this point. Our conversation, once the problems have been addressed, needs to focus on what to do about it.

The present administration, Congress, both political parties, most state governments, and many of the biggest companies in America all

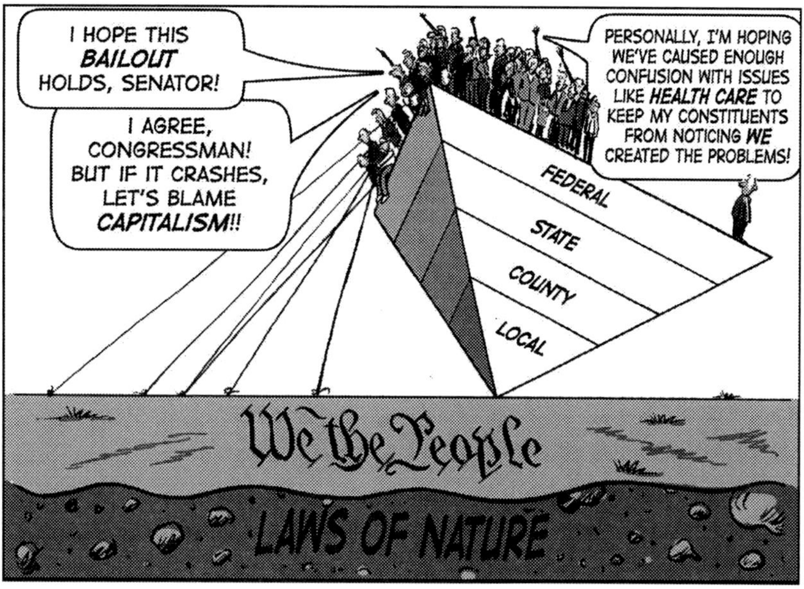

seem to believe we can fix the fundamental problems we face today by continuing to put Band-Aids on symptoms, holding steady on the same track, the same course. But this is the definition of insanity: doing the same thing over and over again and expecting a different result.

In truth, a system that continually violates the laws of nature cannot avoid the inevitable. Anything is possible on a temporary, short-term basis, but sooner or later, the real forces behind these laws will become self-evident. The party ship is on course for a full-on collision, the cause of which has been mostly obscured by smoke, dust, fog, and very muddy, murky waters. At this point, very few have a clear sense of direction and a good, solid idea of what must be done.

For us, as Recovering Federalists, this is a bitter pill to swallow. Like essentially everyone else, we have been riding the wave this country has been on for decades, and we spent a good share of that ride with our eyes shut to reality, completely oblivious to reality, including the laws of nature, and totally naive to what has been going on around us. But we are now ready to open our eyes to the reality of our regrettable situation: The limited and balanced governmental system outlined in the Constitution for governance of the constitutional republic of the

United States of America has been replaced by mob rule democracy, deficit spending, and a corrupt system of political schemes and federal dominion and control, with an intrusive new administrative, bureaucratic branch of government never even mentioned in the Constitution, all run by a ruling elite that delivers marching orders through the two major political parties.

Our Founding Fathers warned us to avoid a welfare state, a police state, gun control, entangling foreign alliances, a grandiose central government, enslaving taxation, paper money not backed by a gold standard, choosing "security" over freedom—and the list goes on and on. Federal politics and big business are getting bigger as state and local governments get weaker and small business is dying. Limited government was the goal, but as a people, we wanted the party without the work. We became willing to trade something *great* for something *now.* It has been said that aside from the color of the slaves, the only real difference between the slavery of today and the chains of bondage of the Old South is that then the plantation owners paid for the chains; today we pay for our own.

At this point, in many ways our federal government has become exactly what our Anti-Federalist Founding Fathers warned against. As Federalists, these words want to stick in our teeth, but having lived it ourselves, as *Recovering* Federalists, we have no choice but to make acknowledgments and concede that they were right in so many ways. Now it's time to do the right thing.

Watch your thoughts, it is said, *for they become words. Watch your words, for they become actions. Watch your actions, for they become habits. Watch your habits, for they become character. Watch your character, for it becomes your destiny.*

We forgot to watch, but we'd better be watching now. We had better watch our words, our actions, our habits, and our character because they are defining our destiny. We have forgotten the laws of nature, but we'd better be remembering them now. One of America's mayors recently said, "We need to move forward, not backwards, with new words and new actions. . . . Words that articulate the same wisdom and principles the founders understood . . . making decisions and taking action with a sound understanding of the principles of liberty and power while adhering to the laws of nature." Neither battleships, aircraft carriers, cruise ships, nor ships of state can turn on a dime. It's going to take time. Are we ready to start correcting course?

Is it Time for *Rehab?*

In this country, as individuals we suffer from a number of well-known, addictive, self-destructive, and dependent behaviors—all kinds of "-isms"—from alcoholism and substance abuse to addictions to sex and pornography. We have also come to suffer from another very addictive and destructive dependency: Federalism—or federal dominion, in accordance with our definition. Again, for purposes of this discussion, it represents the opposite of personal responsibility; it is the concept that government can and should take primary responsibility, and that the federal government should have supremacy, dominance, *dominion,* and complete control in its relationship with *we the people* and the states in this union of united states. Although we may suffer from this addictive dependency as individuals, at this point we certainly suffer from it collectively, as a nation, and when we really stop and look, we can see its devastating effects all around us.

As Recovering Federalists, we have made many acknowledgments in getting to this point. Whether our governments and political parties remain in complete denial or not, as individuals, with personal responsibility in accordance with the laws of nature, we had better not remain in denial. Whether our country, our governments, and our political parties are ready to wake up to reality and make similar acknowledgments about the path we're on may not be entirely within our individual control, but what we do as individuals is entirely within our control.

The whole process starts with recognition and acknowledgment. When enough individuals do this and there is a groundswell of recognition and acknowledgment of reality—including the issues and problems with the current state of affairs—eventually our governments and those who run them will have no choice but to start paying attention and making such acknowledgments as well.

To that end, as noted elsewhere, it is our intention to ultimately develop an organization—a support group—with a rehabilitation program and a support network to help individuals make these acknowledgments in their own lives, squarely address the issues, and find the help they—WE—need in order to straighten out our lives in this country and help fulfill America's destiny of liberty, fostering lasting freedom, peace, and prosperity through personal responsibility, properly balanced/limited government, protection of inalienable individual rights, and sound fiscal policy/accountability, all in accordance with the everlasting laws of nature.

In our next essays, we will provide a more detailed prescription of how to address these issues and meet these objectives. But before attempting to move straight to treatment (which in the past has included mostly temporary Band-Aids), we must first verify the diagnosis and then prescribe the initial, foundational steps that must be taken to prepare for engaging in a proper and effective course of treatment for our governments.

Chapter 8

Another Vision—Another Destiny for America

We have talked about the direction America is currently headed; now let us imagine a new direction. Let's paint the picture of a different destiny, with our laws and our lives consistent with the laws of nature.

In this picture, government at all levels would understand and act in accordance with its proper role(s). Government at every level would understand and respect the inalienable rights of individuals, endowed by the laws of nature and of nature's God. Governments would not attempt to usurp personal responsibility, and they would not attempt to circumvent natural consequences. The single, highest priority of government, at every level, would be to preserve and protect inalienable rights. Instead of a ruling elite of professional politicians at all levels and layers of government, we would have productive and well-qualified citizen lawmakers who know and understand the real world. Elected officials would not attempt to make whole careers out of holding one public office. Some would move on to higher offices while others would look forward to getting back to businesses, real jobs, families, and farms. America would be a strong, independent country with a solid foundation. The foundation would start with individuals and gain much of its strength from families, local communities, and states.

This picture would essentially take the shape of a pyramid—much like a food pyramid. As individuals and families, *we the people* would be the foundation, built on the bedrock of the laws of nature. Individuals would act responsibly, take responsibility for their own actions, exercise their freedom of choice to be productive, exercise good stewardship over resources, and live within their means. And they would be happy

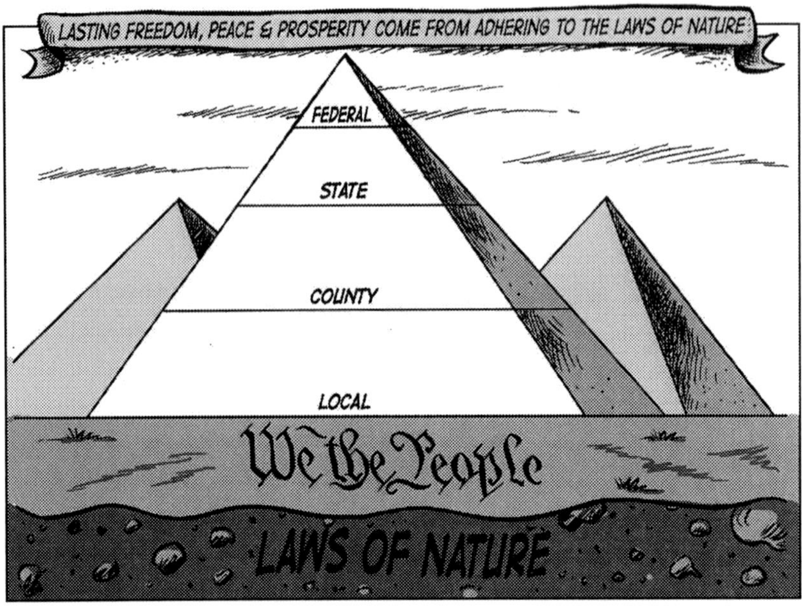

doing it. Families would be close-knit. They would take primary responsibility for everything from production to education, to taking care of themselves and their neighbors. Families would likewise act responsibly, take responsibility for their own actions, live within their means, and take care of their own. Family, friends, and neighbors, not government, would be the cement that holds the social structure together.

Vibrant, productive local communities would be the first layer of government in the properly structured and balanced governmental pyramid. These largely autonomous and self-sufficient communities would be filled with productive, solvent, well-managed businesses, large and small, and would be interdependent with sister communities. These communities would also be filled with safe neighborhoods and surrounded by a wide variety of agricultural producers. Both eating local—locally produced foods—and spending time on neighbors' front porches would become more a way of life than TV watching. Local governments would provide only essential governmental services, live within their means, and endeavor to stay out of people's way. Churches and charities would be robust and active, taking primary responsibility for both helping people in times of need as well as teaching them principles of personal responsibility, independence, and self-reliance. To the extent there were any government "social" or assistance programs, they would be at the lowest level possible. All decisions about such programs would be made, and taxes would be collected and spent, at the lowest level possible, closest to the people. County government would be the next layer in the pyramid.

Strong and well-managed state government, coordinating public safety, transportation, and an effective justice system, would be the next layer. States would also have primary responsibility for most areas of government regulation. But personal responsibility would replace the vast majority of government regulation—on both sides of the equation. Businesses that are not responsible enough on their own would primarily be held accountable by consumers in the market place. Inevitably, some will say this just won't work—some businesses just aren't responsible enough to be allowed to operate on their own. They are just too greedy and corrupt, and they will cut corners or intentionally take advantage of us if government doesn't intervene to keep them under its thumb. In reality, though, the only thing we're really saying when we say things like that is that we don't want to take personal responsibility as consumers, and more important, we simply don't want to be patient enough to let nature, and markets, work and run their course. We want government to intervene, take short cuts to circumvent personal responsibility, and shield us from the natural consequences of everyone's actions because accountability imposed by nature and natural market forces simply takes too long. Moreover, we are under the mistaken belief that all the temporary Band-Aids government applies can and will ultimately eliminate all the pain, when in reality, sooner or later, there's no way around it.

Otherwise, like well-managed community governments, states would likewise exercise fiscal responsibility, live within their means, and largely stay out of the way. They would operate largely as autonomous entities, united with their sister states in a much more balanced system. The federal government would be a true union of the states, with ample respect for individual state rights and autonomy.

At the very top of the properly balanced structure, like sugars in the food pyramid to be administered sparingly, would be the union of sister states known as the federal government. It would not be an empire unto itself and accountable to no one. At this point, the federal government likes to talk about holding businesses, individuals, the private sector, and other governmental entities accountable, but who holds it accountable?

This limited federal government would be solely responsible for national security and defense (supported by state militias and national guards), international relations, coining money, resolving disputes between the states and regulating interstate commerce in a very limited sense, coordination of interstate transportation, a very limited federal justice system, and other duties specifically delegated to the federal government under Article 1, Section 8 of the U.S. Constitution. The Supremacy Clause would apply to those limited roles, and the states and the people, including local communities, would reserve and exercise all other powers.

Neither states nor their citizens would be dependent upon the federal government outside of those limited roles. The federal government would not conspire or compete with business and the private sector; it would operate within a balanced budget and would work to respect and maintain the rights of states, communities, and individuals. It would be a true constitutional republic in a properly balanced system, as government in this country was originally intended to be. "We the People" would have the freedom to succeed or fail at our own hands, to rise from mistakes to fill the measure of success we are capable of through our own vision, ingenuity, hard work, and tenacity.

Foreign relations would change as well. Certainly we would have a strong defense, speak softly, carry a big stick, and be fully prepared to adequately defend ourselves and our allies. But if we're going to accept the fact that we're not an imperial power in the modern world, then instead of continually gallivanting around the globe trying to police other nations, the United States would primarily mind its own business and grant other countries the dignity, respect, and inalienable right of self-governance. Instead of giving out free fish handouts at home and abroad, the United States would encourage people to learn how to fish, to feed themselves primarily through personal responsibility and self-sufficiency. In cases where aid is needed, it would be administered at the lowest level possible, with full accountability, and encouraged and administered primarily by private-sector charities instead of the inefficient federal government. As balance is restored with the states, there would be no need for many duplicative cabinet departments and agencies in the federal government. Less is more. We would return to a properly balanced system of governance, as well as to the commonsense adage—the government that governs least governs best.

As a people, we would be able to pursue life, liberty, and property without fear of interference or competition from federal, state, or local governments. We would be a hardworking, productive, self-sufficient people; exemplary stewards of our natural resources, producing what we consume and consuming what we produce; living within our means, and selling surpluses to our neighbors. We would have and be able to afford health care that makes sense and have reasonable access to an effective justice system that once again focuses on the founding documents and principles of personal responsibility. And as we grow and learn from our experiences and follow the laws of nature, we will experience greater happiness and prosperity. Lasting freedom, peace, and prosperity come from adhering to the laws of nature.

Sound unbelievably rosy? It's certainly no rosier than the picture, spin, and party lines that we've been buying for years. Maybe we've neglected to say enough about all the hard work that will be required to achieve this vision, but we are talking here about a vision of what is possible. We know the world would not be perfect. People, individually and collectively, will always make mistakes and bad things will still happen, even to good people. But when people are held to a higher standard of accountability, and when a people as a whole take a greater responsibility for their own thrift and preservation, people naturally rise higher and thrive more. Again, government's highest priority at all levels is to defend, protect, and preserve fundamental, individual, inalienable rights, including rights of life, liberty, and property, giving us all a greater possibility for advancement and success.

We're talking about the ultimate destiny of America! It is time to cultivate a strong belief in some astounding possibilities. There is much work to do, but work without vision is drudgery. This chapter has been about that vision. But if work without vision is drudgery, in turn, vision without work is only dreaming. Only hope and vision coupled with work equal destiny. What comes next will start to focus attention on waking up and getting to work on fixing the foundation for other important tasks and things we must eventually do to reform our governments and restore proper government balance in this country.

Chapter 9

What Can *We* Do about All This?

We have heard the stories, we have discussed the problems, we have even imagined the possibilities. But where do we go from here? We've been drunk on our federal-dominion wine for such a long time. It's time to wake up, shake off the hangover, and get to work. But once the discussion closes, where do we start?

While it is important to acknowledge where we are, it is even more important to get where we're going. One of our well-known Founding Fathers said, "Any fool can criticize, condemn, and complain, and most fools do." While we haven't been shy about talking about problems, we aren't interested in focusing solely on the complaints. This book—the reason for writing it—is not just about highlighting core problems; it is also about suggesting solutions consistent with the laws of nature. What can we do to correct course? What can we do to fix the foundation? While we fully intend to explore these questions further in upcoming essays, the purpose of this essay is to lay the foundation.

In 2008, a new president was elected. His election was viewed as a major event, promising change in America. But change is not effected easily. And there is always the question of just what kind of change is really needed. Right now, this year, in 2010, the entire U.S. House of Representatives and one-third of the Senate are up for reelection—what a golden opportunity. Is that the place to start? It is certainly an opportunity that should not be ignored or wasted. Many people believe the only way to make a meaningful difference in this country is to start at the top.

But we believe the first and most important place to effect real change is at the bottom—right at home—at the foundation. Before undertaking the major task of reforming our governments, we must first undertake the task of reforming ourselves, individually and collectively, in preparation for reforming our governments. We must start at the very foundation. It would be a huge mistake to ignore the foundation in favor of top-down solutions. That is what has been going on for decades. It is our unwavering position that top-down national and global approaches don't work *for the good of the people. We the people* need to be the first to stand up, take responsibility, and rely on the bedrock of the laws of nature to start fixing the foundation. Although restoration (or establishment) of balance between state and federal governments in our *Federalist* system is critical, the mismanagement of some states shows why we need to start at an even lower, more basic, foundational level to truly fix the foundation of this great nation. It is critical to our future and our ultimate destiny.

We need more than minor tweaks, and we need it at every level. We are beyond the point of cosmetic face-lifts or "fixing the roof." We must rebuild from the bottom up and fortify the foundation that made us strong in the first place. Government is not the foundation, *we are.* With the laws of nature as the bedrock and the Constitution as our tool, *we the people* are the foundation of this great nation and its very existence, and we are the ones who must plant our feet on solid bedrock and rebuild from there.

When we understand and stick to the laws of nature, there is no need for the discussion of action steps to be particularly long or complicated. If we get into a discussion and debate about values, morals, and social issues—things that could be debated endlessly without agreement—we probably won't get anywhere. But it's pretty tough to argue with or about the laws of nature. Consequently, it will be our objective to advance positions that are always consistent with the laws of nature.

Vision is seeing what others don't. Faith is doing what others won't. Relying on faith with vision, we need to take back true liberty. To that end, the following section is arranged in two parts: "What We Need to Be" and "What We Need to Do"—right at the most basic level where everyone finds themselves. In upcoming essays we will address specific steps that need to be taken to address core systemic issues and problems in our governments and political system, including discussion of substantive governmental policy and structural changes. But before we do that, we must first look at ourselves. These steps are the beginning of what we hope will be a growing list of faithful and visionary *actions.*

What We Need to Be: A List of Attributes for Fixing the Foundation

One of our great aims in life should be to develop character. Character is composed of self-esteem, self-discipline, the ability to delay gratification, and the willingness to accept full responsibility for our lives and everything in them.

The more we say to ourselves, "I am responsible," the stronger, better, and finer person we become. And every part of our lives will improve at the same time. Here are some attributes that will help us in the process.

1. **Be Informed.** We as a people have been lulled to sleep. We have become distracted and apathetic and have turned a blind eye to a government run amok and a country on the edge. It's time to wake up and sober up. It is imperative that we see past the spin that surrounds us and get interested and educated in a very proactive way. We need to get informed on a deeper level. We must be willing to spend less time Facebooking and more time studying. We should know both history and current events, but not just the mainstream propagandist spin that we are fed by dominant media sources. We should read and understand the words of the Founding Fathers. We should know the Declaration of Independence, the U.S. Constitution, the amendments, and even the Federalist Papers. We should study enough to gain a solid understanding of the historical basis for what has happened in this country and around the globe. We have time for *LOST;* let's devote some time to getting found.

As we learn more, we need to be bold enough to share it with our friends and neighbors. While some may not be ready to hear about these issues, many will be ready to join us in the occupation of self-education and prepare to act toward the good changes that need to occur.

2. Be Committed. We must consider the laws of nature and how they apply to us *today.* In all likelihood, we have all been part of the problem up to this point, and we need to examine ourselves and make some painful admissions. As the writers of *Bedrock!,* we are in the process of doing plenty of soul-searching ourselves. But once we acknowledge our part, it is time to set our sights firmly upon the horizon, commit to the changes that need to be made, and step forward to make them. Together, we must remove the rose-colored glasses of so-called patriotism, throw off the shackles of party politics, and be willing to be honest about the current state of the State and our role in apathy; then it is time to forgive each other and ourselves and move on toward building a better future.

3. Be Positive and Proactive. *Whether we think we can or we think we can't, we're right.* Instead of being reactive, we need to step up with optimism and be proactive. We must believe we can make good things happen and *act.* They say there are three kinds of people: those who make things happen; those who watch things happen; and those who wonder what happened. We need to be the ones making things happen. With persistence and positive action, we can each make an effective and important difference.

4. Be Sincere. The vast majority of our politicians and elected leaders tell us exactly what they think we want to hear. There is nothing real about many of them or their messages, which change with the audience. We need to be different. We need to be real and we need to be realistic. We need to be sincere, truthful, flexible, and adaptive while staying true to the laws of nature that apply to everything and working toward making a difference without the hype or promises typical of the political arena.

5. Be Productive. Being productive means many things. It means being a net producer instead of a net consumer. Do we produce more than we consume? Make more than we spend? Make positive contributions? Do we bring positive, productive energy to the situations we face? Productivity is an attribute of good results. Productivity means we are willingly engaged in moving forward at every opportunity, in every way presented. Productivity increases goods and it increases good.

6. Be Self-sufficient and Self-sustaining. We can't accomplish much as long as we are dependent. The more dependent we are, the more vulnerable we are. This applies to us individually, as families, as communities, as states, and as a nation. Food, finances, and energy are significant challenges of dependency for us as a nation. Imported money, imported food, and imported oil and energy sources are all handicaps we face. But we change that first at a personal level by taking more personal responsibility. Individually, there are many things we can do to develop greater independence and self-sufficiency. We start with simple things and take one step at a time, getting back to basics. We live within our means. We save for a rainy day and pay down debt. We contribute to our own food supply by growing a garden or prepare for the unexpected by storing extra food and water. Walk, ride a bike, better insulate our home, install a solar panel. Most important, we need to learn and develop practical and productive skills that are useful in a variety of situations, environments, and economies. We must address the reality that we, as a people, are almost completely dependent on technologies and infrastructures that may not always be available or helpful. We need to learn how to take care of ourselves.

7. Be Neighborly. We need to practice the golden rule. Get to know the family across the street. In our busy world, we seldom take time anymore to write a note or hold a neighborhood barbecue, but these are the things that build strong communities. Smile. Wave. Lend a hand. Notice the people in your neighborhood and learn their names. We need to take more than a passing interest in people. This is the only way a movement can begin, and it's on the neighborhood streets of America. The transformation will not be effected in council meetings or boardrooms; it will begin between neighbors, over fences, around dinner tables. Our neighbors must be our friends before they can be our allies.

8. Be Tough. Be resilient. Disregard the dissenters. Our goal is not popularity; our goal is growth. What we are working on is so much greater than we are. Life and liberty cannot be minimalized by power-hungry elites. We will not let the prospect of conflict, contention, or controversy stop us from doing what is right.

9. Be Persistent. An entire system of governmental domination will not change overnight. It's going to take time. We can't do the work in a day. But if we are persistent, taking small steps, doing the right thing over and over again, making small decisions count, we will succeed. If we find that what we are doing isn't working, we will adjust and move forward again and again until we achieve the transformation we envision. Never quit. Practice makes perfect.

10. Be Tenacious. The road to restoring liberty, personal responsibility and properly balanced government will not be short. It will not be smoothly paved. It will not be easy. This run is a marathon, not a sprint. As we seek to draw our country away from the edge and turn the corner, slowly changing and evolving our country into the republic it was meant to be, we'll need to develop patience. There will be times when the changes are difficult to see. Tenacity and patience, along with the consistent, faithful execution of all the attributes we have listed, will conquer. We *can* effect the positive, lasting, sustainable revolution we seek.

What We Need to Do:
A List of Actions for Rebuilding From the Bottom Up

1. Stand Up. Once we have made the effort to get informed, we have to take a stand. As we come to understand the political collusions and misdeeds, we can no longer be indifferent. We must take a position, roll up our sleeves, and get involved. Seeing where we are headed is not enough. Many people are aware of these issues; they may talk or philosophize about them, but many have been unwilling to back their misgivings with action. Many more find themselves willing but unsure of what steps to take. The time has come for us all to stand up and act. We all must be ready to do something bigger, even, than just writing a letter to a congressman or sending an email to city hall. The letters and emails should continue, but they are not enough. To change the course of our history, it's going to take more.

2. Take Personal Responsibility. What does personal responsibility mean? It means we acknowledge and take responsibility for our mistakes along with our successes. We hold ourselves accountable and accept the natural consequences of our actions, both good and bad. We take care of ourselves and take care of our families, learn to be productive, and learn to live within our means. Personal responsibility means we must get our own houses in order before attempting to get the world in order. We must change ourselves before attempting to change the world. And we further that change by taking responsibility for making something happen beyond our own lives and across our country without waiting for someone else to do it.

3. Take Action. As we discuss what we need to do, perhaps the question whose answer eludes us most is *how* do we take action? What do we *do?* The first step, individually and as families, groups, and communities, is to make a plan. Take thorough stock of where things stand in our own communities. Then make a plan to address the issues and problems that present themselves. Visualize a desired goal, prioritize what must be achieved in order to better your community, and then list and prioritize the steps that will be required to get there. As we continue this discussion, we will talk about things that ought to be on that list. But once a plan is made, we need to follow through and *do* something. We need to *work* our plan. We can't be afraid to make mistakes. In fact, we can't afford *not* to make mistakes. That is how we learn. Failure is a prerequisite to success, and practice makes perfect. Can we outline every step as we are just beginning? No. We can't learn to walk until we first learn to crawl. We must decide together how to create the transformation we seek. We will define and build together the revolution we deserve.

4. Get Back to Basics. The laws of nature are the bedrock of our existence. The first, most fundamental action step we must take—and the one step that could actually encompass all the others—is to bring our lives, our actions, and our decisions into alignment with the fundamental commonsense laws of nature. The laws of nature are not a thing of religion; they transcend philosophical debate or political opinion. They are fundamental truths that exist before all other schools of thought or belief. Although we often try to make this very complicated, it is, in fact, quite simple. The laws of nature simply *are.* When we allow ourselves to stop examining and resisting this, we can exert phenomenal growth and success in our lives by doing this one thing: living in accordance with the laws of nature. This is the most basic and important course of action of all. As we practice being aware of the laws of nature, bigger steps that we can implement on a larger scale will present themselves, and our understanding of what we need to do will increase.

5. Prioritize. Most of us have become habitual multi-taskers—and many of us are under the delusion that it works! With all that ails this country, we probably won't have much success if we attempt to tackle it all at once. We need to prioritize. We need to define the most critical issues and further define the core causes of, and obstacles to, change. For some, these will be local issues. Others feel there are state or national issues that demand the most attention. As Recovering Federalists, we have not drawn a conclusive list. Our goal is to instill in ourselves and others an urgent desire to discover these priorities and join together in a persistent effort toward their achievement. What are the priorities for you? What do you need most? We must decide and prioritize, then choose our battles wisely and focus our efforts on winning those battles. That is how we will make progress.

6. Work Together. No matter how much we can accomplish on our own, we can accomplish so much more working together. The sum is greater than its parts. This is especially true when it comes to the kinds of public policy changes that are needed in this country. We are all different, with unique strengths and gifts. When we each use our talents, we work more efficiently. Recruit, join, and support one another; work together and help make each other better and fully capable of handling the tasks at hand.

7. Strengthen Our Communities. Although the biggest problems are arguably in Washington, D.C., that is not the most important place to start. Until we do something to take back and strengthen our communities and then our states, all the big rallies and million-man marches in the world aren't going to accomplish much more than a cloud of dust. We've got to get down to the core causes. We've got to do the real work that is necessary to *fix the foundation.* One step at a time, from the bottom up, will yield results. But new legislation or new faces in office are not the *first* results we seek. The place to start has to be in our homes. We need to develop and strengthen our personal and family friendships and relationships and then work outward into our communities, counties, and states.

Areas that deserve particular attention are local economy, local food production, local energy production, and local government and political reform. Then we need to strengthen our states, particularly in their relationship with the federal government. We need to strengthen our state and local economies by buying local, eating local, and networking for local energy production. We need to educate ourselves in ways to boost state and local production and efficiency in all areas. In order to make major political and economic changes in Washington, D.C., we need to first make political and economic changes at home.

8. Hold Government Accountable. In theory, politicians and elected leaders are directly accountable to us—*We the People*—but in reality seldom are. Accountability has become elusive for several reasons, not the least of which is administrative red tape, which clogs and backlogs a system, making it easy for officials to pass the buck. But another reason accountability is virtually nonexistent is simply that we have allowed it to be so. We are often indifferent to proposed changes, ill-informed about proposed legislation, and uninvolved in development even at the local level. Many of us neglect even to vote!

Most candidates for office are party-loyal rather than principle-based and will say and do anything to get elected, often forgetting their constituents until it's time for reelection. Letters and e-mails from citizens, therefore, can't compete with party bosses or the corporate pocketbooks.

But in the end, it is we the taxpayers who support the government. The current system of spend-now-make-someone-else-pay-later would never make any sense in the private sector, and we need to stop it. We need to insist that government live within its means at all levels.

This begins with throwing out labels. Letting party labels like Republican or Democrat do the thinking for us is a serious mistake. Although they paint themselves as black and white, red and blue opposites, the reality is, they all operate in the same gray zone.

Mainstream media is co-opted in all of this, their message almost completely dictated by the two major political parties. Independents and third-party candidates get little or negative recognition. We need to look past these mainstream messages and past the spin to find the truth, both about issues and about the candidates and leaders themselves. Become principle, not popularity, based. Get educated. Go to city council meetings and county commission meetings. Most of us are completely uninformed, especially on a local level, where it really counts. Unless we see it on the nightly news or hear it around the water cooler, we're completely in the dark.

Get to know your elected officials and make sure they know you. Support them in good decisions and be vocal about bad ones. In today's world where "good is bad and bad is good," it can be lonely for an elected official making right decisions as they relate to exercising fiscal discipline, adhering to the laws of nature, protecting property rights, and limiting government. When they do a good job, let them know. Most decisions are made with virtually no input from the people they will affect. In order to hold government accountable, we must first hold ourselves accountable to understand what is going on.

9. Elect Better Leaders. Our friend Worth likes to say, "It's only 90 percent of the politicians that give the rest a bad name."

Many candidates for office say exactly and only what they think we want to hear, making it difficult to know who might actually do the work they promise and represent us well. Instead of getting sucked in by all the spin, we need to look at their fruits. "By their fruits ye shall know them." What kind of fruits of their labors do they bring to the table to show for their decisions, actions, and judgment? How many of our elected leaders truly possess sound judgment? Well-qualified people are often kept from office by smear campaigns or media manipulation, leaving professional, career politicians who are little more than party-led puppets on the ballot.

Instead of politicians, we need statesmen. We need to raise the bar and search out good, well-qualified, *citizen* lawmakers who are already active in productive professions and trades and are not seeking to make a career in politics. Good candidates need real-life experience *outside* the political arena. Rather than flattering résumés, degrees, and credentials, we need men and women with sound principles, uncommon common sense, sound judgment, and enough backbone to stand up to big business and party bosses. Men and women who know what it's like to make payroll and keep a company in the black, who have learned from the school of hard knocks and even failed a time or two. We need leaders who have figured out how to apply the right principles and become successful through life lessons.

In short, we need real people from the real world who are willing to say no to the party line—people willing to make hard decisions in order to live within the means available. At the end of the day, *we the people* need to wake up, stand up, and start taking back our government by being a lot more particular about the people we elect to public office—nominating and electing principled leaders who possess sound judgment. In evaluating candidates, possession of the following attributes would be a good place to start:

- Strong commitment to the concept that the single, highest priority and paramount purpose of government at all levels is to protect individual, inalienable rights based on the laws of nature.
- Demonstration of a fundamental understanding of the laws of nature and the importance of personal responsibility, along with a commitment to apply such principles.
- Demonstration of a solid understanding of the Constitution of the United States and any individual state they serve, including properly balanced government and a commitment to abide by such constitutional principles.
- Commitment to preserve liberty by making government—at all levels—more transparent and accountable to the people while defending and protecting the inalienable rights of individuals, including life, liberty, and property.
- Commitment to hold the body in which they serve, and any others they have oversight for, financially accountable by balancing applicable budgets, with no allowances for financing of general government obligations and operations through debt.
- Commitment to declare all conflicts of interest, and not participate in any votes or discussions involving any matter from which they

receive any direct benefit (including large campaign contributions, gifts, and so forth) to themselves, their immediate family, or their business interests.

- Commitment to seek to limit government rather than enlarge it, and to seek proper balance between the levels and branches of government.
- Commitment to reduce and simplify new legislation based on the recognition that we already have an overabundance of unnecessary laws.
- Commitment to prioritize principles over party and principles over politics.

Upstanding candidates for public office should be willing to make such commitments and abide by them, even after they are elected and exposed to all the corrupting influences that seem to overwhelm elected leaders and the system they operate in. If, after being elected, they cannot keep these commitments, they should not be reelected.

10. Keep Moving Forward. Just as there were for the revolutionary patriots and the Founding Fathers, there will be stalls, dead ends, and setbacks along our recovering path to personal responsibility in accordance with the laws of nature. There are many ways we can act, many facets to a plan for reform, but the most important thing is to keep moving forward—keep searching for the next step, keep finding toeholds as we make the steep climb to liberty, personal responsibility, and adherence to the laws of nature. We can't outline every item that will need to be accomplished along the way, but if we keep moving and keep watching, the next step will always present itself.

Putting Theory Into Practice—Just One Example: The Rest of the Matt James Story

When Matt James left the stock brokerage where he worked in Chicago to return to the farm, half his colleagues chided him, said his brain had turned to mush, and couldn't believe what he was doing. The other half told him in secret that they envied him.

As described earlier, Matt's path was not always an easy one. Although he had been a successful stockbroker, he had a lot to learn when it came to making do on less and surviving on the farm. Although Matt watches government carefully, his initial focus was on getting his family's house in order and helping others do the same. One of Matt's big concerns is just how unproductive and dependent we have become. He is concerned about the growing lack of basic, useful skills. Moreover, Matt doesn't have quite as much confidence in our government and the existing industrial agricultural system as many people seem to. He does his best to make sure that he and his family are always in a position to take care of themselves. They believe in local production and local consumption. They believe in self-sufficiency and independence. In addition to the other farm products they produce, Matt and his family grow a big garden. They also have a very practical small greenhouse and share much of their produce with friends and neighbors. They have also recently added solar panels and a wind generator, which allow them to meet many of their own energy needs and sell any excess back to the local power company. Matt and his family practice what they preach and encourage others to do the same.

But even more important than what Matt and his family did is what happened next. Although for a time, because of financial struggles, Matt was almost embarrassed to talk to any of his former stock brokerage colleagues, eventually he developed a successful niche selling healthy, farm-fresh products directly to his former colleagues, friends, and clients in the city, who were happy to know where their food was coming from and have a direct connection to the farmer who grew it.

Eventually, as a result of positive word of mouth, demand for Matt's products outgrew what he was able to produce and provide with a personal touch. At that point, instead of attempting to further expand his own operation, Matt started helping some of his former friends and colleagues develop their own food production right in the city and suburban communities where they live.

Matt helped one friend plan and develop a neighborhood garden, with individual plots for each family to tend. He helped another friend organize, plant, and harvest a community potato patch. It seemed like a good place to start. They found a large, vacant lot and made arrangements to use it. They solicited contributions to buy enough seed potatoes to plant the entire lot. Then they put the word out that anyone in the community could come help plant the potato patch, weed and care for it over the course of the summer, and share in the harvest in the fall. Dozens of people, including several families, showed up to help plant the potato patch, and the planting went remarkably fast. Rows were assigned for weeding, hilling, and other responsibilities for the summer to ensure a good harvest. That fall, there was a bumper crop of potatoes, and everyone pitched in to harvest them. It was a big job, but many hands make light work, and before they knew it, they had mounds of potatoes available for those who had helped to bag up and take home. After everyone who helped had taken all the potatoes they wanted, there was still well over a ton of potatoes left over! The extra potatoes were donated to a good cause. The first season was a huge success. The following year, the response and turnout were even better, and that year the new gardeners planted carrots, melons, and sweet corn as well.

Matt's biggest, noncommercial local community food production project to date was helping yet another friend and his associates in another state organize and develop a small raw milk dairy co-op in his suburban community. Although they shared the belief that there are health benefits associated with raw milk, their main motivation was self-sufficiency. There wasn't a dairy within fifty miles of their community, and the milk in local stores came from much farther than that. In addition to the security of knowing exactly where their milk came from and how it was produced, they were also concerned that a wide variety of events could interrupt the supply of milk and other dairy products to local stores.

With Matt's assistance and direction, they organized the co-op by recruiting twenty households, ranging from large families that consumed ten gallons of milk a week, to empty-nesters and widows, who might use only a quart or two a week. Together, they pooled money in a tiered structure based on how much milk each household anticipated using. With the pooled financial resources, they found a suitable place to rent for housing the small dairy operation, retrofitted it for the intended purpose, bought three beautiful Brown Swiss milk cows, equipment, and enough feed for a year to get started. They then organized a milking schedule, relying primarily on responsible teenagers in the group to take turns milking the cows and doing chores in exchange for a fair and reasonable wage. In addition to receiving milk, many of the co-op members learned how to make other dairy products, including cheese, butter, ice cream, and yogurt with extra milk that was occasionally available. Based on their success, they also decided to add an egg co-op to their venture. Although no such ventures are without challenges, these co-ops proved to be successful, and are still in operation. Fortunately in this case, although they are continually concerned about new federal regulatory developments through the USDA, at least the laws in their own state allow them to organize and do what they are doing.

Obviously, Matt's story and example may be of no interest and have no application to many. But it is just one example of what can be done. And it's a great example of what just one person can do to make a difference. What Matt has learned is that often it only takes *one person* to catch the vision and run with it, and soon others will follow. Judging by his experience, that is a recipe for success.

We intend to include other examples of what people have done to get informed, be proactive, stand up, and take action, politically and otherwise, in our upcoming essays, particularly *Enough!*

PEOPLE OF THE REPUBLIC: STOP YOUR FIGHTING! LEARN TO ADHERE TO AND APPLY THE LAWS OF NATURE... THEN YOU WILL KNOW HOW TO CLEAN UP THIS MESS!
Laws of Nature
Laws of Nature
YAY!
HOORAY!
FEDERAL
STATE
COUNTY
LOCAL
THUD!

Chapter 10

It's Entirely Up to *Us!*

After all is said and done, we can wrap this up pretty quickly and rather simply. Another saying from our friend Worth fits the bill: "Getting things done is awfully simple if you know how; simply awful if you don't."

In this essay, we have barely scratched the surface of what can be done. While it looks like the process may be pretty complicated, it's really not. It begins with adhering to the laws of nature. First adhering to them in our own lives, and from there working together as families, neighbors, communities, and states to hold our governments accountable to both *we the people* and to those irrefutable natural laws to which all things are accountable. Only then can we put our governments back in their proper places, in their proper roles, on a solid structural foundation, constitutionally.

As we have illustrated, when there is no equity in a home, the owner has little incentive to hang on. It's natural because there is little financial incentive to stay and no value to fight for. On the same basis, and in accordance with the laws of nature, the simplest way to deal with many of the abuses and excesses we see in government is to simply stop funding them. If there are no financial incentives to further grow the empire, nature will take its course. There will be a corresponding double bottom line: life will be better and we'll start digging our way out of the hole we're in.

Many will inevitably say it's already too late to address the core causes, or it's too much work. And, inevitably, some will be afraid it will cause too much pain. In fact, so many people are so far removed in their thinking and actions from the laws of nature that they will be fearful to return to the fundamentals discussed in this essay.

To those who assert that the laws of nature are simply too painful, we would remind them of the pain and devastation that occur when the dam breaks and when the ship sinks. We can keep trying to take shortcuts as individuals, families, communities, and as a nation. We can continue violating the laws of nature, asserting that we are doing it to avoid temporary pain and discomfort, but when we do, we fail to recognize and acknowledge the pain and failure that will inevitably come when nature finally catches up with us. As Worth says, "Everything has its cost, and sooner or later someone will pay."

We believe that we are immeasurably better off to recognize our mistakes and get to work to uncork the dam ourselves. Remember: "What wise men do in the beginning, fools end up doing in the end." The strength and stability this will bring back to us as individuals and families, as well as to our government, will be worth the work. Think of the hope and liberty this will bring back to America! Think about what it will mean for our children and grandchildren. They will be free to choose their destiny, rather than having it imposed upon them by the ruling elite, enslaving debt, and government bureaucrats who tell them what they may and may not do. America can once again be a home of the free, productive and brave.

Let us tell one last story to illustrate this point. Worth tells of a rancher who was in a bind, short of help, and desperately in need of a new ranch hand. When a man came along looking for work, the rancher tried to quickly quiz him about his qualifications, but he was in such a hurry to put the new man to work that what he said barely sunk in. The only thing he said that the rancher remembered was, "I can always sleep when the wind blows."

Although it didn't make sense to the rancher at the time, he put the man right to work and thought no more about it.

The new hand seemed to be doing his job and taking care of things, and all was going along pretty well. Then one night a big windstorm came up. The rancher woke up in a panic. He thought of all the things he hadn't done—all that needed to be secured and tied down to prevent damage or loss. He ran to the bunkhouse to wake the ranch hand and get his help. As the rancher shook him and tried to rouse him, all the ranch hand mumbled was, "I told you I can always sleep when the wind blows." In frustration and panic, the rancher ran out into the wind and dust to make sure that everything was safe and secure, but everywhere he ran, it was already done: the barn door was securely fastened; the ladder was tied securely in place; all the gates were secure; all the animals, tools, and equipment were accounted for; everything was safely in its place and tied down tight. The ranch hand had made sure that all this was done before he went to bed. Suddenly, it all made sense to the rancher: "I can always sleep when the wind blows." With that pleasant revelation, the rancher was able to go back to bed himself, thankful for a ranch hand who had done what it took to be able to sleep when the wind blows. By paying attention, being responsible, and taking care of some very simple tasks every day as he went along, rather then leaving them all for later—always hoping that it wouldn't come back to bite him—he prevented much bigger problems.

The same is true for us in this country, but we as a nation do not have a reliable ranch hand. We have to do the work ourselves. At this very minute, and for at least the last few years, we're running around in a panic, trying to get everything tied down before it all blows away. Somebody has to do what it takes to get things tied down and make things secure again.

Where can we find such ranch hands? There's only one place: right here. We need to look in the mirror. It's up to us. We need to wake up from our drunken stupor of federal dominion, make the necessary acknowledgments, and start taking control of our lives and our country. We've been sipping the Federalist Kool-Aid long enough. They say once an alcoholic, always an alcoholic, but we are ready to recover. We are ready to leave our addiction and our dependence behind and go through whatever work and pain are necessary to gain back our liberty. No longer convinced of the Federalist agenda, we have awakened to become *Recovering Federalists.* It may be tough to stay on the wagon, but we're going to do it. We've got to do it. We are well-acquainted with the alternative, and we know from personal experience that things have to change.

What's it going to take? After getting over our hangovers, we've got to start undoing and unwinding things just the same way they happened. We've got to catch the vision of what can be. We've got to draw that picture, put plans on paper, and then start implementing those plans. This will all require action and a lot of hard work. It's the kind of work we didn't used to be afraid of in this country, and it will require some relearning of skills. But it's necessary and critical work, and it's work we can do. The vision of a strong, self-sufficient, and truly independent republic can be ours again! We can take back our government and our liberty! We can restore our country to the bedrock and rebuild this great nation in accordance with the laws of nature as it was meant to be! We can still, after all this, recover. Lasting freedom, peace, and prosperity come when governments are accountable to the people who created them and recognize the need for proper balance, personal responsibility, and adherence to the laws of nature.

There's much to do. Let's get busy!